THE LADDER OF VISION

Irma Brandeis has been for a number of years professor of literature at Bard College and a member of the Liberal Arts Faculty at the New School for Social Research. Miss Brandeis received her B.A. from Barnard College and did graduate work in comparative medieval literature at Columbia University. She continued her studies in Italy, where the late Dante scholar Mario Casella first urged her to publish her interpretation of certain cantos of the *Inferno*. She returned to Florence in 1955 on a Bollingen fellowship for the completion of the present book. Her writing has appeared in a number of magazines, and she has edited a collection of essays entitled *Discussions of Dante*. Two sections of *The Ladder of Vision* appeared originally in the *Hudson Review*.

THE LADDER
OF VISION

A Study of
Dante's Comedy

Irma Brandeis

Since, then, one must climb Jacob's ladder before descending it, let us place the first step of the ascent far down, putting the whole of this sensible world before us as it were a mirror through which we may pass to God. . . .

ST BONAVENTURA

ANCHOR BOOKS
DOUBLEDAY & COMPANY, INC.
GARDEN CITY, NEW YORK
1962

In memory of
NICHOLAS KALTCHAS

ACKNOWLEDGMENT NOTE

The author of this book owes debts of gratitude to many persons for their assistance and encouragement: to Barbara Deming, especially, for her patient readings and even more patient counsel, and to Joseph Campbell, Guido Di Pino, the late Helen Huss Parkhurst and Paolo Vivante. She would like also to acknowledge the generous assistance of the Bollingen Foundation.

The text of the *Comedy* quoted in these chapters is that of the Societa Dantesca Italiana, edited by Scartazzini and Vandelli, edition of 1955, Milan.

The English translations of Dante's works are, except where otherwise noted, those of the Temple Classics Edition, J. M. Dent, London, and E. P. Dutton, New York. Translations of other foreign works, when not credited in the footnotes, are by the author.

Quotations in Chapter headings

Chap. I. GEORGE ELIOT: *Worldliness and Otherworldliness.*

Chap. II. A. N. WHITEHEAD: *Science and the Modern World;* Macmillan Co., 1925.

Chap. III. *The Teachings of the Compassionate Buddha;* ed. by E. A. Burtt; The New American Library.

Chap. IV. Ibn Arabi, quoted in A. J. ARBERRY: *Sufism;* A. Unwin, 1950.

Chap. VI. PLATO: The *Timaeus;* tr. by B. Jowett.

Title page epigraph from SAINT BONAVENTURA: *Itinerarium Mentis in Deum.*

Two sections of this book (chapters II, b and V, a) appeared originally, in substantially the same form, in *The*

Hudson Review (Copyright 1953 and 1956), to which acknowledgment is made for permission to reprint them. Acknowledgment is also made to T. S. Eliot, Faber and Faber Ltd. (London), and Harcourt Brace (New York) for the quotation from *Selected Essays* on pp. 143–144.

CONTENTS

THE LADDER OF VISION

INTRODUCTION

In 1922 Benedetto Croce electrified all readers of Dante, and outraged the majority of them, by writing a book in which he announced that the *Comedy* was not, as most persons had so long supposed, a whole and integrated poem, but rather a "theological romance", spiced by occasional passages of true (and here he meant lyric) poetry. Such unity as the work has, he said, is structural; and its structure grows from a purely practical and didactic motivation: to represent and to teach about the world beyond death. The unity of the *Comedy* and its poetry, therefore, are separate matters: the first is incapable of telling us anything about the second. It follows that all study of the action of the book, of its concepts, or of its protagonist, is quite irrelevant to the poetic experience.[1]

The value of this pungent attack was that it put forward certain fundamental questions in such a way that no one interested in Dante could quite ignore them. Dante critics, especially, were shaken out of their beatific assumption that all this had been settled long ago, and forced to return, temporarily at least, from the antipodes of scholarly commentary and elaborative description, to the primary question of poetic substance. Readers of the *Comedy* had to face the logical possibility that Croce was right, and the book not so much a poem as a demonstration of heavenly judgments and arrangements for the afterlife. And those from whom the name of Dante's poem drew a sigh of total admiration were invited to ask themselves just what it was

[1] B. Croce, *The Poetry of Dante* (Henry Holt, 1922), tr. by D. Ainslee

they sighed for: lesson? fiction? lyric patches? or poem?

The present study, although it is not a theoretical argument but a series of textual studies designed to show the ways in which Dante's meanings are fused in his images, hopes to demonstrate the answer, *poem*; and, integrated poem; thus, whole poem, without any dissidence between structure and other elements.

The structure of the *Comedy* is not, as Croce would have it, a representation of the otherworld; to think that it is, requires that one overlook its plot and its protagonist. The structure of the *Comedy* is a representation of a quest conducted in the otherworld, laid before us as the quester's memory dictates, when the journey is over. It is literally a voyage through Hell, Purgatory and Heaven and, allegorically, a search for understanding of the order and nature of the universe, projecting a moral geography of the soul and a Christian examination of the soul's wanderings from and return to God. All these are closely knit by the strictest threads of symbolic imagery and dramatic action; indeed, they are developed simultaneously by a writer who at times seems grandly careless whether his reader can be expected to catch all his shades of meaning and interlockings of themes.

Clearly if this is an accurate description, the structure of the *Comedy* is not "didactic"—or certainly not in the sense which opposes this word to "poetic". Poems do teach; poems lay hold of men's lives and profoundly change them. But they do so as images of truth and by the avenues of feeling, and not as intellectual persuasions. The *Comedy* is undoubtedly in this sense a poem and not a lesson. If any doubt arises, that is because its plot, concerned with an *education*, puts the reader at certain points in the presence of intellectual and theological arguments where he is apt, at first, to be bogged by the sheer difficulty or unfamiliarity of the content. To meet the book on its true ground one must get past this point. For the poetic action of the *Comedy* can be fully experienced only when the reader begins to *feel* the demonstrations which are offered to the intellect, and to *understand* the actions which appeal first to feeling.

By demonstrations offered to intellect I mean those expositions and lessons in ethics, cosmology and metaphysics which make up the greater part of what Croce considers non-poetry. It is true that one is likely to balk at these in one's first meeting with the *Comedy*. How, one may well ask, does the time of day in Hell or Purgatory—announced in so many and such roundabout statements of the hour on earth—enter into the "poetry" of this vision? Who cares, struggling with the facts of damnation, whether the sun is standing in Scorpio or Aries? But on second reading one begins to feel these risings and fallings of stars and sun; they remind the reader, they remind the voyager in the realm of spirit, that he belongs also to the realm of time, and that the landscape under the literal sun has justly precious harmonies and changes of lights and seasons.

Or one might ask how poetry is served by Statius' discourse on human generation, or by any of the many doctrinal passages based on Aristotle or Thomas Aquinas. The answer is that these passages—which, to be sure, have no lyric or dramatic value out of context—mark the moments in which the pilgrim-protagonist, who is essentially a learner undergoing an immense schooling, turns from his instruction by immediate experience to draw on the stored knowledge of the cultural tradition. He must hear his teachers out in full because his mind is still awkward and full of misconceptions, while the reader must hear them out because there is no other way of following the true development of Dante's plot. And these lessons, too, are intended to be felt rather than construed by the reader, however much he may have to study them before he is able to receive them in this way. Each is an image of the mind in action, fed by tradition and by speculation.

The engaging dramatic scenes of the narrative present a much subtler problem to the reader who would see the *Comedy* as an integrated poem. Independently fascinating, they have frequently and conspicuously enticed readers and scholars into forgetting what the book is really about.

Some of these scenes—for example, the meetings with Paolo and Francesca, with Brunetto Latini, with Count Ugolino—have in fact become quite famous for their detached poetic or dramatic beauty. When this approach is taken, the profound and exquisite relevance of these scenes to the large scheme of the *Comedy* is lost from sight, and one fails to see that each is the image of a psychological or spiritual process in a linked series. Thus Croce, who was guilty of this shrunken view, could say of such passages: "Each one of these episodes stands by itself and is a lyric by itself,"[2] as though their actors were attached to the regions of suffering and correction by the mere tether of a heavenly decree. But he was wrong. Far from being pauses or "asides" from the great themes of the poem, such scenes stand at the real heart of the matter. It is not too much to say that each has been deliberately fashioned to reveal in dramatic form the essential nature of some particular moral condition; each carries forward the work of the whole poem as cogently as do the revelations by argument, by dream, by sacramental vision.

Every portion of the poem and every kind of matter in it—"didactic", dramatic, symbolic, lyric—enters into its central theme of the human condition defined in terms of its freedom and its dependence, and into the central image of a journey from the misery of un-knowing to the bliss of vision. Each portion yields its own images or systems of interrelated images. These are so intricately woven and over such a length of cantos that one has at the beginning the impression of an endless, receding vista to be explored. But there is a point of acquaintance for every seriously interested reader where it is possible to stand off from the poem a little and sharpen one's eyes for a broader view; and from this perspective it is clear that Dante's images spring all from one centre, or circle round it in many connected strands, forming a single brilliant web. The essays in this book are an attempt to follow the movement and composition of a few exemplary strands.

[2] Croce, *op. cit.*, p. 92

Chapter I

SUBSTANCE AND IDEA

Now emotion links itself with particulars, and only in a faint and secondary sense with abstractions. . . . Wherever abstractions appear to excite strong emotions this occurs in men of active intellect and imagination in whom the abstract term rapidly and vividly calls up the particulars it represents, these particulars being the true source of the emotion; and such men if they wished to express their feelings would be infallibly prompted to the presentation of details.

GEORGE ELIOT

The reader of Dante's *Comedy* has acutely the sense of being in touch with an inviolate conviction that the world is meaningful: not a tale told by an idiot, but the utterance of a noble god.

In the middle of the twentieth century, when such a conviction is not ours any more and we have become expert at saying why, this may be all the more moving to us. But we would be wrong to suppose that Dante drew his certainty as an easy deduction from his own life, or from the human conditions he saw round him in a remote and comfortable age. It would come closer to the fact to say that he arrived at it, in an extremely troubled age, only after painful lapses and bitter struggle (as the adventure of the hero in the Dark Wood suggests); and that he held it in spite of acrid distaste and disappointment. His poem has in it the prophetic rage of an Isaiah. It is at times lashingly angry and rough and bitter. But beyond the rage and resolving it, it has the Socratic detachment which comes of finding that the ways of things make sense and that truth is an assertive force however men persist in obscuring it.

The idea of the world as a theophany—a shifting play in time and space of tangible forms, each realizing some infinitesimal portion of the divine immaterial principle—was not new when Dante wrote. He may himself have encountered it in certain works of the Arabian Sufi poets. He saw it forecast in Thomas Aquinas' doctrine that the ideas of all things existed in the mind of God in anticipation of the Creation, and were by his will made manifest. St Bonaventura had suggested it in his description of the Creation as a ladder by which we mount to God, discovering him diversely mirrored in each rung. Simpler lessons from such teachers as Honorius of Autun and Hugh of St Victor had read the life of each beast and plant as a living allegory. And the poet Guido Guinizelli had recently touched off in northern Italy a whole new lyric school based on the conception of human beauty as bearing an imprint of the divine. All of these were attitudes that took the world as consecrated. What they offered to Dante, who came after them and had in mind a different sort of book, was support to his conviction of a rational and harmonious order underlying the chaotic document of human experience, and encouragement to his sense that the world's facts are suffused with meaning. The document, he knew, was jumbled and blotted by man's hand; the facts, if one tried to pry out of them some knowledge of human fate, seemed opaque. But he was sure that a patient reader could still make his way back to what the original author had intended, and find the sense of what now seemed obscure. It is this that the hero of his *Comedy* —as poor a reader as a man can be, when he sets out on his journey through the otherworld—achieves through the disciplines and revelations of the way.

But there is a difference between Dante and those other

writers with whom he shared belief in a god-revealing universe, and it lies in the degree of his concern with the
substance (rather than the fact, alone) of the theophany.
The things of the world, both material and ideal, both as
they seem and as they are, engage his mind and his
feelings; they are his teachers. So that one is aware in the
Comedy of an attitude quite new in poetry: a profound
concern with ideas equally balanced by an intense interest
in the actual world, and above all in the concrete expressions of men's lives.

This at once puts Dante at a great distance from
Aquinas and the other philosophers or theologians from
whom he borrowed for the rational scaffolding of his poem.
It makes him properly speaking a poet—a creator of images, not systems of ideas. It results in a work which is
philosophic in texture but not in method, and which is
centred on insights into experience rather than dogma.

This dual concern also sets Dante beyond the poets of
the lyric school in which he had learned his craft, by the
sheer breadth of his interest and the depth to which he
questions it.

And it separates him radically from the conventional
allegorist, whose only interest in the flesh that encloses
his personified or objectified ideas is that it points the
reader beyond itself to the truth it encloses. The Cardinal
of Capua who wrote about roses that they were

> the chorus of martyrs or the choir of virgins—either
> red with the blood of those who died for the faith, or
> white for virginal purity, hedged round with the
> thorns of heresy or of iniquity[1]

was not really concerned with those flowers, but saw in
them a pretty puzzle to be solved, and a device for edify-
ing the simple. And Guillaume de Lorris, whose more so-
phisticated flowers had become ladies without features,
was scarcely more interested in the people of his story as
people. But Dante's eye is always fixed first and last on the

[1] Quoted in Émile Mâle, *L'Art religieux du XIIIième siècle en
France* (Paris 1931), p. 30

object in which meaning or virtue is vested. It is fixed with
burning love and with insulted love on man and his action
in the world, and does not shake off the burden of their
image until he has covered the vast distance of his journey
between "Florence and a people just and sane".

Nothing tempted Dante to minimize the strong impact
on him of the world's stern and powerful, though often
deceptive reality. Real things, real persons are his starting
point: himself and Beatrice in the *Vita Nuova*; and in the
Comedy these two at a different point of time, together
with a large cast of characters modelled from life, and as
many places, objects, landscapes, all meticulously observed.
Dante resembles Homer, whose work he never read, in the
range and immediacy of his characters; and he reminds
one often of Shakespeare in the depth of his quick psychological insights. He does not intend us to think of something else—something beyond—when we look at the stage
he sets; and we cannot do so, because his actors are so
acutely there in themselves and satisfying in themselves.
Unlike the characters of standard allegory, they do not
point to but precipitate meanings. Or one might say,
Dante's meanings are *in* the things of his poem, qualified
by the dense individuality of those things, so that we
must take note of everything and discount nothing in order
to grasp the meanings. If this is allegory at all, it is allegory of a totally new sort, in which the concrete terms of
the story no longer refer us outward to abstract concepts,
but are incandescent with undetachable meaning in every
part.

To be sure, some comparable relationship between substance and idea is achieved in other great poems. But it is
unique in Dante's work because the theme itself of the
poem concerns the association of substance and idea in
human life. The whole dramatic dialectic of the work is
based on the clash Dante sees between man's immediate
(or substantial) goals and his final and ideal one, acted
out in the human consciousness with its responses of suffering and joy. Man chooses not merely to do or possess
this or that, but to possess happiness in consequence. But

because he is subject to fits of blindness and hallucination with regard to the things he desires, and cannot easily tell the ingredients of happiness from those of pleasure, his immediate joys are apt to block him off entirely from his final one. The truth in things eludes him, and he freely selects the path that turns out to lead to his own wretchedness.

How is he to do better, when his own errors hedge him in? Evidently he needs assistance. And were he able to see with his own eyes all of experience under its eternal aspect, so that he could know the path and outcome of every human impulse, his happiness and goodness would follow certainly. It is such a view that Dante chose to provide for the hero of his poem.

By luck the notion of a concrete three-part otherworld—Hell, Purgatory, Heaven—lay ready to hand for his purpose—traditional matter, matter of belief, yet a subject which up to now had been given only the simplest and crudest of pious representations in the Christian west. He had also, from the teachings of Aquinas, the touchstone idea that the souls in the otherworld are as they were in their lives. From this spark, very likely, came Dante's whole crucial conception of the otherworld as an ordered reflection of the life in this world. And this suggested that if a living man could reach the afterworld, he would see a panorama of the souls of men withdrawn from all their vital disguises as well as from their chance groupings according to time and place—souls with the essential modelling of their wills made evident in their action, and with the degree of their insight into the truth shown by the nature of their destinations along a vertical scale from damnation to bliss. For that living man the voyage and the study would make his eyes what they ought to be—not a sensual organ but an instrument of the mind, whose business it is to discover the essences of things under their superficial and perishable coverings before his time comes to see them in their single, absolute source.

In some such tenor of thought the plot takes shape. A man, we are told, is lost in a dark and savage wood. He

tries to escape—to reach a sunlit hill which is visible in the
distance—but is held back by three threatening beasts who
silently press him backward and downhill. Miraculous aid
comes to him in the ghostly person of a beloved poet and
teacher. He learns that he cannot be saved from his pre-
dicament except by exploring the whole dark abyss to
whose edge he has stumbled. With the help of his rescuer
he makes this journey through Inferno, observing the conditions of the unrepentant sinners and talking with many
of them. He emerges from the darkness and pain of that
abyss and climbs upward, with constantly increasing comprehension, along all the paths of correction of error that
make up the mountain of Purgatory. Finally, healed
through the exercise of reason and imagination, he is re-
united with the beloved lady through whom he had caught
his first glimpses of truth, and with her help sees the life
of perfected being. At the end of the journey he is in a
position to look back on human life in the perspective of
eternity, and on his own strayings in the light of his goal.
For an instant he glimpses the whole piecemeal universe
at one in God. He returns to the world in the free serenity
of clear discrimination and infallible love.

The outlines of this story spring from the underground
chamber of familiar myth. Like Adonis and Osiris, Odys-
seus and Aeneas, the hero of the *Comedy* enters the country of the dead, undergoes experiences that equip him with
new powers, and returns into the sphere of his first life.
To die and to be reborn: this is an old story, endlessly repeated in legend, ritual and the records of individual psychological experience; and it holds the reader with a claim
on his imagination that asks no justification from reason.
Whether it touches ancestral remembrances—as Carl Jung's
theory of archetypes would suggest—or a less profoundly
buried awareness of forces capable of impelling the living
spirit of a man towards death, and of others capable of
restoring it, the pattern is familiar and understandable to
every adult.

Intimately bound up with this first mythic pattern is
another that links the hero of the *Comedy* with all hunters

for the Golden Fleece, the plant of life, the waters of life, the Holy Grail—adventurers who set out through strange countries on difficult missions, face and survive dark dangers, and return home bearing some holy object or peculiar knowledge which is the key to life-renewal.[2] The specific circumstances of the journey may be new to the reader, but the road itself will seem to him one he has travelled before, time out of mind, and not in books alone; it is a reprise of old and inward experience.

Over this skeleton of myth is cast the solid body of the literal story: the hero's long journey through the otherworld, his encounters and lessons, his growth from an abject creature, stupid with fear and wretchedness, to the stature of a man who knows the measure of his motives and his deeds. There is scarcely a moment in this text when we do not feel vitally aware of the regions through which the story takes us—their dimensions, substances, colours, motion and the souls that inhabit them; so that at first Dante's hold on us seems to come exclusively from the brilliance and wonder of this supernatural fiction.

But soon the poem begins to carry us beyond its immediate objects into another dimension of perception where the journey, for example, of the lost man downward into Hell becomes that man's—or any man's—cautious and perilous venture into the darkness of his own soul. And presently the whole solid world of Hell, without losing its solidity, begins to make itself felt as a series of stages of the spirit representing the destinations of the living rather than the dead. We find that the souls of the dead, drawn so sharply in portraiture, reveal to us nothing but the essential traits which have shaped them. We see that the souls in this landscape get their peculiar vividness, their lifelikeness, not from a rounded modelling according to the look of life, but rather from the fact that they have been pared of every single extraneous trait. Thus everything Dante tells us about them leads in the one direc-

[2] For a study of this pattern see Joseph Campbell, *The Hero with a Thousand Faces* (Bollingen-Pantheon, 1949), especially Part I, chap. IV.

tion of showing us the relation in which they stand towards their happiness; which means towards the truth; which, in turn, means towards God. And the various ditches, terraces and spheres of the three otherworld regions are the true locations of these souls along a spiritual scale that begins in incomprehension, at Hell's narrowest point, and ends at an elevation from which all landscapes are brilliantly comprehensible.

The process of winnowing the literal story, the things seen and heard in the journey, for the silent meanings with which they are brimming, does not end here; nor is it possible to say where it ends. Always the scene arrests us first and holds us continuously, urging its significance more and more through its tone, its web of interconnected strands, and the universal image that the entire book is building. And more and more as we become aware of the significance, we find the literal narrative illumined in reflex, the literal text flooded with fresh power. For its images have an expansive capacity which their meanings seem unable to exhaust; their tensile strength and suppleness are capable of holding in suspension a whole world of rational and emotional significance.

If, now, we attempt to take this integral and musical work apart—if we try to examine its images and abstract its ideas separately, it is in the hope of seeing a little more clearly the intricate paths which the poem pursues as one thing, and which we must eventually follow as one. We shall reach only approximations; and never any guarantee of their justness. The *Comedy* will survive that. In the end, all the meanings of Dante's poem will be found intact in its images, and the images intact in their setting, impervious to mishandling by time or criticism.

Chapter II

THE IMAGE OF SIN IN ACTION

Evil is the brute motive force of fragmentary purpose,
disregarding the eternal vision.

A. N. WHITEHEAD

(a) FRANCESCA

Inferno, Canto V

In 1922 Father Giovanni Busnelli remarked acidly about
Dante's Francesca da Rimini that she had been talked
about "in various ways perhaps more than any other soul in
the *Comedy*, by writers, novelists, dantists, commentators,
lecturers and libertines".[1]

He was right, I am sure, although certainly powerless to
stop this flow; for the heroine of the first great sin-defining
canto of the poem continues to attract every reader so
strongly that not even the peril of finding oneself at the
wrong end of Father Busnelli's terrible list acts as a deter-
rent; and the last word yet remains to be said about a lady
of whom it is written that:

> ". . . she keeps her soul immaculate; she preserves
> that indefinable softness, purity, delicacy, which con-
> stitute the truly feminine . . ."[2]

and

[1] G. Busnelli in *Miscellanea Dantesca*, ed. by Paduan Catholic
Committee, Padua, 1922
[2] F. De Sanctis, *Lezioni e Saggi su Dante* (Turin, 1955), p. 640

"Her fault is purified by the ardour of her passion,
and truthfulness beautifies her confession of desire"[3]

while conversely it is said that she is

"the demoniac woman who employs her fair person,
her sensual charms, to bemuse the virtue of the gentle
heart and lead it to perdition"[4]

and that her words betray

"the urgency of her fault and of her desperation, her
obstinacy in sensual perverseness, and the outbursts
of an immense rancour."[5]

This is perhaps a frivolous beginning for a grave subject.
But it is also serious; for these quotations are perfectly exemplary of the main tradition in the criticism of Dante's
characters, and the essays from which they come may as
well be posted in warning against the easy error of con-
fusing a work of art with a work of life, and of evaluating a
literary character without taking stock of the evaluation
already incorporated in it by the author. These four writers, in spite of the difference that pits two against two,
have one great bond: a context-blindness that makes it
possible for them to separate Francesca from the scene
Dante has wrought so carefully around her, and causes
them to look at her as though she were a detached portrait
made from life, and they her interpreters. They forget that
she is not a woman but a soul in Hell; they do not notice
that Hell means something of which she must be an in-
tentional expression, nor that she is one figure in a dialogue
which as a whole is planned to tell us something about the
action of love. Because it is very easy to fall into these and
other traps of unwary reading, I should like, before turning to the text itself, to outline three general points which
it may be helpful to hold in mind throughout the *Inferno*.

[3] U. Foscolo, *Discorso sul testo della Commedia di Dante*
(Genoa 1930), p. 101
[4] G. Trombadori, quoted by M. Barbi in *Vita e fortuna di Dante*
(Florence 1952), p. 185
[5] G. Busnelli, *op. cit.*, p. 54

First, that the hero of the poem has just emerged from a dark wood of spiritual error. Everything he does and says is characterized by his as yet unimproved weakness. If the reader confuses him with the Dante who writes the story at the completion of his educative journey, he misreads the text and loses the sense of the encounters in Hell. The author of the poem is not in Hell; he is in Italy, presumably full of experience and reflection, and he is the conscious creator of the childlike and troubled figure of his earlier self who walks by Virgil's side. He is very careful to separate that pilgrim's voice from his own voice, when he wants the poem to affirm some judgment of his mature thought.

Second, that the members of Dante's Hell, having died impenitent and come directly into the afterworld, bear their sinfulness with them and are, as we see them, exemplary of it. Indeed, since the soul is all that survives and the sin has characterized the soul, one does better to take *all* that Dante reveals as concerned with the sin, than to suppose him capable of forgetting where the pilgrim is and what the conditions are which he himself has posed. His dramatic situations are not lapses from his subject; they are his moral subject given in images of action. The theme of moral error is never lost from sight in the *Inferno,* although the reader must often search it out in its protagonists. What misleads many readers is the fact that Dante reveals human sinfulness without destroying its essential quality of secrecy.

Third, that the members of Hell do not know that they are sinful, however well they may remember that they have committed a formal breach of moral code. Knowledge of sin implies repentance as precisely as knowledge of error with respect to some scientific truth implies correction. Repentance, had it occurred in life, would have carried the penitent to Purgatory. If, instead, we find the soul in Inferno, we must assume that it is ignorant of the real cause, and therefore incapable of expounding it. The pilgrim, being also in Hell, is not much better off. We have

therefore no right to assume that Dante's evaluation of
carnal sin, or any other, is to be found either in the explanations offered by the inhabitants of the abyss or in the
emotions of the hero.

The poetry of the second Circle of the *Inferno* is from
its beginning an interplay of opposite elements, paving the
way into the two-faced tragic emotion which its dramatic
episode is to arouse. In the opening section the atmosphere
is a contrast of warring winds and soft, blown figures, of
harsh curses and "doleful notes", which the verse supports
with its alternation of rushing, bellowing, lashing sounds
(28–36) and its passages of dulcet music (40–41, 46–49).
The dramatic scene will carry out these contrasts in its
counterpoint of passion and pity, of cherishing weakness
and destructive power, both generated by love.

Out of the black air the spirits emerge, first as voices
weeping, lamenting, blaspheming; then as visible shapes
borne on the wind:

> *E come gli stornei ne portan l'ali*
> *nel freddo tempo, a schiera larga e piena:*

And as their wings bear along the starlings, at the
cold season, in large and crowded troop:

and

> *E come i gru van cantando lor lai*
> *facendo in aer di sè lunga riga,*

And as the cranes go chanting their lays, making a
long streak of themselves in the air,

These two bird images do more than tell us how the
figures look: they suggest innocence and lightness; they
flood the harsh atmosphere with softness, and lure the
reader's memory away from the curse against the divine
power uttered by these same powerless shadows. The impression the images create will be reinforced by line 73,
the pilgrim's first view of Paolo and Francesca as "those

two that go together, and seem so light upon the wind";
and further by the image of line 82:

> *Quali colombe dal disio chiamate,*
>   *con l'ali alzate e ferme al dolce nido*
>   *vegnon per l'aere dal voler portate;*

As doves called by desire, with raised and steady
wings come through the air to their loved nest, borne
by their will:

and ambiguous lightness and ambiguous gentleness will
run through all the crucial scene that is to follow.

But we are in Hell. The poet has not forgotten that; nor
ought the reader to be able to, since the context within
which these images appear is a hellish storm, whirling and
smiting. The storm, if we read the poem's symbolism, is
the externalized image of an inner tumult against which
these souls, *as though they were innocent and frail*, have
lacked resistance. But to be innocent means to be unaware of the problem of evil, to which man has been
bound since Adam exiled him from Eden. And Dante tells
us in several ways that these souls were not unaware; he
calls them "the evil spirits", he shows them blaspheming
the divine power, he defines them as "those who subject
reason to lust", and he names among them heroes and
heroines of legend whose uninnocent stories he expects his
readers to know: Helen, Achilles, Tristan, Dido. When,
against this background, he compares the motion of Paolo
and Francesca to the flight of homing doves (doves, the
birds of Venus), he throws further into relief all that in
which they are or ought to be *unlike* birds: deliberate
choice, memory, remorse.

Those who subject reason to lust are all like and unlike
doves. They are, as Mario Casella puts it, "the conscious
and voluntary victims of pure feeling, which is the work of
nature; they are victims of love interpreted as the human
will intent, according to nature, upon the good of the subject, alone. . . ."[6] Victims of pure feeling—and as such

6 M. Casella, Canto V dell'Inferno in *Lectura Dantis* (G. San-
soni, Florence 1940)

we all yearn towards them and forgive them; but human, thus responsible to reason—and as such we are rationally compelled to admit them to Hell. Neither they nor we, however, see so far during the unfolding of Dante's scene. They can only regard the wind that pains them with horror and grief. They are sorry for themselves. They are shut up in their sorrow, unable to escape it by turning their attention to those others whom they involved in blood and grief. Francesca will speak of her and Paolo's condition as "our perverse misfortune", not out of rancour, but because that is all she can make of her situation. That, and the fact that the King of the Universe is not their "friend". We on our part pity them through our human identification with their love-longing. But if we do not block our ears and eyes we shudder simultaneously, for we hear the inevitable storm headed our way. So the poem plunges us into the tragic emotion: pity and terror aroused together by a twin insight into a single situation.

In the prelude to the central scene, troops of souls are whirled past the spot where the pilgrim stands, and Virgil points out "more than a thousand" "whom love had parted from our life". Of these Dante repeats to us the names of some half-dozen, all conspicuous in legend and literature. His list is intentionally full of alluring magic: Semiramis, Dido, Cleopatra and the rest. (Since not all, even of these, died as a consequence of love, we must assume that the poet meant that the life of each was spoiled by love—love always as desire dominant over reason. The implication is that love, pitted against reason, inevitably destroys— Helen, who did not die, as much as Tristan; and Paris as much as Dido.) Moved by pity and "bewildered", the pilgrim looks at this vast airy host and singles out a particular pair who go together, very "light upon the wind". It will not be difficult to speak with them, Virgil says: he has only to call them, invoking "the love that leads them, and they will come". Virgil knows. Love (as *amor*) is the key, here; love is the only language understood.

The pilgrim obeys. One may easily suspect that he is himself smitten with the infection of this circle, for he calls out with an "affettuoso grido" of such power that it at once arrests the wind-borne pair. And the wind, allowing them this pause, grows silent for them.

The words which are exchanged here merit the strictest attention. "O wearied souls! come to speak with us if none denies it," the pilgrim calls. They come, and Francesca answers:

> "O animal grazïoso e benigno
> che visitando vai per l'aere perso
> noi che tignemmo il mondo di sanguigno,
>
> se fosse amico il re dell'universo,
> noi pregheremmo lui della tua pace,
> poi c'hai pietà del nostro mal perverso."

"O living creature, gracious and benign! that goest through the black air, visiting us who stained the earth with blood:

If the King of the Universe were our friend, we would pray him for thy peace, seeing that thou hast pity of our perverse misfortune."

88–93

These words, her first, are warm and personal to a notable degree. Like so much else in the canto, they have a double scope. They suggest the anguished loneliness of the wind-swept life—for they are a very large response to a small "affettuoso grido". But at the same time, by their tone, by their adjectives—"grazioso" and "benigno"—by their use of the intimate *thou*, they cradle the stranger's instant pity and they suggest in Francesca a rather quick compliancy. And this compliancy is the very nature of the soul that goes by her name, and the root of her sin.[7]

The pilgrim, too, is compliant. He reaches out towards Francesca with his pity and his tears because he is like her in amorous weakness, is still in the shadow of the Dark

[7] Some readers may not accept this association of compliancy with sin. Says F. De Sanctis, speaking of Francesca: "The poetry of womanhood lies in being conquered." Such a view, however popular, cannot be found in Dante.

Wood, and differs from her only in that Virgil stands guard over him, and his repentance is still possible. He is identified with Francesca in the overwhelming tenderness of their feelings so clearly expressed in this canto, in their thoughts centred on love, in the suavely laden language of love which both employ. The very sounds of their speech suggest their openness, their unresistingness. "O anime affanate!" (O wearied souls) cries the one in greeting; and "O animal grazïoso e benigno" (O living creature gracious and benign) the other replies; while "Amor che al cor gentil ratto s'apprende" (love which is quickly caught in gentle heart), spoken by Francesca, might just as suitably have been printed in the thoughts of the young man who stands languishing before her.

Briefly Francesca tells the pilgrim all he needs to know in order to identify her and recall her story: where she was born, the theme of her life (ineluctable *amor*), her treacherous murder.[8]

> "*Siede la terra dove nata fui*
> *su la marina dove 'l Po discende*
> *per aver pace co' seguaci sui.*
>
> *Amor ch'al cor gentil ratto s'apprende,*
> *prese costui della bella persona*
> *che mi fu tolta; e 'l modo ancor m'offende.*
>
> *Amor ch'a nullo amato amar perdona*
> *mi prese del costui piacer sì forte*
> *che, come vedi, ancor non m'abbandona.*
>
> *Amor condusse noi ad una morte:*
> *Caina attende chi a vita ci spense.*"

"The town where I was born sits on the shore where Po descends to rest with his attendant streams.

Love, which is quickly caught in gentle heart, took him with the fair body of which I was bereft; and the manner still afflicts me.

[8] The grim story of this murder was familiar throughout Italy.

Love, which to no loved one permits excuse from loving, took me so strongly with delight in him, that, as
thou seest, even now it leaves me not.

Love led us to one death; Caina waits for him who
quenched our life."

97–107

There is a doctrine of love expressed in this speech, and
it is roughly this: that love for a fellow-creature is an irresistible force set in motion by physical beauty. Not
merely does it take sudden hold and absolve no one who
is loved from loving in return, but it is the master of action, for it led Paolo and Francesca to their death. Paolo
fell in love with Francesca's "fair body", and she with his
piacer—a word which would be correctly rendered in this
text by *charm* or *beauty*, but which, because it signifies
literally *pleasure*, suggests also the possibility that Francesca fell in love with Paolo's love for her. In her whole
discourse throughout the scene there is, in any case, nothing that suggests a view of love which ranges deeper into
the causes of love than the *fair forms* pleasing and attract-
ing and mirroring one another. These instigated the love,
brought about the fatal kiss, and are now eternally joined
as shades in the windy spaces.

The intimate attraction of personal love, the sense of
helplessness under its magnetism which this speech em-
phasizes and which her final speech raises to higher powers, are all that Francesca knows; they dominate the scene
in its entirety, they are the sources of all its lightness and
gentleness, and they are apt for the moment so to engage
the reader's sensibilities that he, too, feels them uncriti-
cally. But we do not by any means grasp all Dante's intention in his statement of them until we reread the episode
in the context of the larger doctrine of love which the
whole poem unfolds, little by little, and which is not complete in any part. The *Purgatorio*, especially, where the
human struggle is still foremost, echoes with reminders of
Francesca that suggest the fatal narrowness of her conception. Beatrice, standing at the opposite end of the scale

from Francesca, knowing equally well the power of "the fair members wherein I was enclosed",[9] will know also that the fair person on which Francesca so concentrates is the merest lure—the first rung of the ladder of love, pointing the way forward to other steps, but in itself perilous to cling to, and fruitless. And the pilgrim will recognize in himself the error from which Francesca still suffers in Hell, namely the blinding to a greater value by the charm of a lesser—the charm of "present things with their false pleasures".[10] Virgil will say to Statius: "Love, kindled by virtue, hath ever kindled other love",[11] and his qualification will point up the shallowness as well as the self-exonerating motivation of Francesca's "Love which to no loved one permits excuse from loving . . ." But most important of all the lights the *Purgatorio* throws back on the second circle is Virgil's answer to the crucial question: if the soul's whole action is correctly defined as love, and if the soul is helplessly open to the appeal of external things, how can it be blamed for "falling"—or praised for refraining? Virgil answers that, in effect, it cannot be blamed for any inclination whatsoever of natural appetite, for in this it has no choice. But

> *innata v'è la virtù che consiglia,*
> *e dell'assenso de' tener la soglia.*

> *Quest' è il principio là onde si piglia*
> *ragion di meritare in voi, secondo*
> *che buoni e rei amori accoglie e viglia.*

innate within you is the virtue which giveth counsel, and ought to guard the threshold of assent.

This is the principle whence is derived the reason of desert in you, according as it garners and winnows good and evil loves.

Purg. XVIII, 62–66

[9] Purg. XXXI, 50–51
[10] Purg. XXXI, 34–35
[11] Purg. XXII, 10–11

This means that although the impulse of love towards any of the world's fair forms is truly not a matter of choice, human judgment and human will have the power to reject or accept, to turn away or to yield.

Francesca is damned, not for loving her fair brother-in-law, but for falling into his arms against a better judgment, and thus "staining the earth with blood". (But actually I ought rather to say that she is damned *by* than *for* her action, since the whole demonstration of the Inferno shows its sufferings as resulting from its sins. One cannot stress this too much: it is a cardinal advance in Dante's thought over all naïve theology in this area that he takes the sinfulness of sin to lie in its destructivity, and its destructivity to be its whole punishment.) Had either Paolo or Francesca heeded the "virtue which giveth counsel", they would never have kissed. Nothing could have been more natural than that they should not have heeded it—as Dante is aware—but the natural is no barrier to man's misery, since it is of the essence of his being to remember and to reflect, and memory and reflection permit judgment and correction of human nature. What hurts Francesca in Hell is not an external tempest, a punishment imposed from outside, but the inner tumult of her painful choice, the storm of sensual desire closed in upon itself by the adulterous circumstances in which it arises; and it is the storm of remorse turned inside out: not for her sin against life, but for the only things she knows how to feel concern with—her own death, Paolo's death, and the ending of their embrace. Their embrace *is* ended; it is the irony of Hell that she is bound for eternity to an exceedingly frail shadow, who in the whole scene before us can only weep in silence. That *amor* of which Francesca says "even now it leaves me not", has become through their living embrace utterly barren.

Present things with their false pleasures—her own fair form and Paolo's—close Francesca's view to any wider horizon. Unable to restrain the action of a love to which the circumstances of her marriage denied sanction or scope, she hugs that limited, personal, possessive passion which is the essence of Hell. She feels that her fair form was cruelly snatched from her; this act of murder still irks her (*e il modo ancor m'offende*), although her own offence which invited the murder goes unrepented and, indeed, unmentioned. She is linked to Paolo's ghost by her own deed—futilely, without prospect of growth or change.

If, however, Francesca is impenitent—as are all souls in Hell—there is no element of deliberateness in her fault. Inferno does not mature the soul, does not make it aware of what it is, even through the stretches of eternity. Unwittingly, Francesca is what she was: a falling lady—an impulsive lady who falls because she is compliant, and whose compliance bends to the immediate and personal desire, without consultation of reason and without ear for its reminder that her love infringed on other sacred bonds in a context far wider than the personal. I take this to be Dante's meaning in the scene he gives us. She does not know who the pilgrim is and does not, as other souls will, ask; she yields to the temptation of his interest and pity and tells him her whole story, betraying all her sweetness and weakness without disguise or suspicion. If the reader, pitying her, wishes her out of Hell, let him note that Dante considers this the human thing to do: the pilgrim does so, too. If the reader thinks that she *ought not* to be in Hell, that is another matter: Dante is telling us not what he thinks ought to be, but what he thinks *is*, and showing us why certain human choices, impulsive or deliberate, have painful consequences.

What Dante sees and reveals in this brief episode is not altogether unlike what Tolstoy shows us at length in the disintegration—which has the same sense as damnation— of Anna Karenina. For not only the pathos of Anna's love but also the certainty and the quality of her suffering relate her closely to Francesca. Her adultery, a blind act in itself, lays an impossible burden on her capacity to look squarely at reality—so that the darkness characteristic of Hell is perfectly familiar to her. And eventually the "fair forms" which have meant nothing to her at first come to dominate her whole thought: imagining that Vronsky is bound to her by her youth and beauty alone, she concentrates all her energy on maintaining her attractiveness—her face, her figure, her style, her charm—with a success that only increases her despair. When she begins to take laudanum, and to cultivate the admiration of every sort of hanger-on, never escaping from her terrible preoccupation, she is already a full member of the second Circle.

Dante's pilgrim is in danger, too. Facing Francesca, he is aware of no fault whatsoever in her, except possibly the technical one of the adultery. He is all feeling without judgment, both as respects Francesca and himself, and it is easy to see that in her place he would have done exactly as she did. His bent head falls when he has heard her first speech to its end. Virgil is obliged to rouse him out of this absorption, in which his thoughts have been filled with tender and personal curiosity about these lovers, about their "sweet thoughts", their great desire and the occasion of its fulfilment. Then, with tears of grief and pity, he questions Francesca, and his words, laden with sensuality, show more strongly than ever how his own perilous inclination matches hers:

> "*Ma dimmi: al tempo de' dolci sospiri,*
> *a che e come concedette amore*
> *che conosceste i dubbiosi disiri?*"

"But tell me: in the time of the sweet sighs, by what and how love granted you to know the dubious desires?"

118–120

Upon these words Francesca, because the pilgrim has "such desire" to know, accepts the pain of articulate remembrance and, in twelve peerless, compact lines condenses the events and emotions of the day that shook the lovers into each other's arms.

> "*Noi leggiavamo un giorno per diletto*
> *di Lancialotto come amor lo strinse:*
> *soli eravamo e sanza alcun sospetto.*

Per più fiate li occhi ci sospinse
quella lettura, e scolorocci il viso;
ma solo un punto fu quel che ci vinse.

Quando leggemmo il disïato riso
esser baciato da cotanto amante,
questi, che mai da me non fia diviso,

la bocca mi baciò tutto tremante.
Galeotto fu il libro e chi lo scrisse:
quel giorno più non vi leggemmo avante."

"One day, for pastime, we read of Lancelot, how love constrained him; we were alone and without all suspicion.

Several times that reading urged our eyes to meet, and changed the colour of our faces; but one moment alone it was that overcame us.

When we read how the fond smile was kissed by such a lover, he, who shall never be divided from me,

kissed my mouth all trembling: the book and he who wrote it was a Galeotto; that day we read in it no farther."

                                                        127–138

The pilgrim, listening, seeing the silent Paolo's tears, swoons with pity as the canto ends.

So necessary is this final swoon that even the most trivial reader is apt to hesitate a moment before he makes the mistake of smiling at it. For the love which this whole scene defines is itself the swoon of amorousness pursuing no end beyond itself. The whole canto is faint with its goal-less sweetness, couched in mellifluous verse, in melting tenderness, in soft images which silence momentarily even the terrible background of tempestuous winds. But the tempest will put an end to this pause and resume its prey, as Francesca knew when she agreed to speak with the piteous stranger "while the wind, as now, is quiet for us". Caught up in such yearnings of the unreasoning, covetous heart, the scene seems to say, either one swoons into oblivion, or one is blown off into the round of Hell.

(*b*) FARINATA

Inferno, Canto X

The shade of Farinata degli Uberti, an illustrious Florentine Ghibelline who had died a year before Dante's birth, rises up to accost the pilgrim from one of the chest-like flaming tombs of the Heretics as the two travellers cross the rough-paved sixth Circle. In the descending scale of evil their place is just below the four circles of the Incontinent and above those whose heavier sins of Violence and Fraud had "injury" as their goal. They have fallen further away from intellectual and divine light than those who lie above, in that there is deliberation in their sin. The reader learns from Virgil that the section where the pilgrim has paused to look about him is reserved for the Epicureans, who "make the soul die with the body", and infers that Farinata is one of these. He may take the tombs to signify the voluntary, painful self-burial of the soul that rejects immortality. He is prepared by earlier encounters with the shades of the dead for the pilgrim's modest curiosity which launches the scene, and for the poet's swift, penetrating revelation of character, for the historical and human interest of the episode, for the precision and strength of the language. But there is something else here which underlies and determines the interest of all the rest.

22   "*O Tosco che per la città del foco*
        vivo ten vai così parlando onesto,
        piacciati di restare in questo loco.

        La tua loquela ti fa manifesto
        di quella nobil patria natio
        alla qual forse fui troppo molesto."

"O Tuscan! who through the city of fire goest alive speaking thus decorously; may it please thee to stop in this place.

Thy speech clearly shows thee a native of that noble country which perhaps I vexed too much."

28 Subitamente questo suono uscìo
   d'una dell'arche; però m'accostai,
   temendo, un poco più, al duca mio.

Ed el mi disse: "Volgiti; che fai?
   Vedi là Farinata che s'è dritto:
   dalla cintola in su tutto 'l vedrai."

Io avea già il mio viso nel suo fitto;
   ed el s'ergea col petto e con la fronte
   com'avesse l'inferno in gran dispitto.

E l'animose man del duca e pronte
   mi pinser tra le sepulture a lui,
   dicendo: "Le parole tue sien conte."

Com'io al piè della sua tomba fui,
   guardommi un poco, e poi, quasi sdegnoso,
   mi dimandò: "Chi fuor li maggior tui?"

Io ch'era d'ubidir disideroso,
   non lil celai ma tutto lil'apersi;
   ond'ei levò le ciglia un poco in soso,

poi disse: "Fieramente furo avversi
   a me e a miei primi e a mia parte,
   sì che per due fiate li dispersi."

"S'ei fur cacciati, ei tornar d'ogni parte"
   rispuosi lui "l'una e l'altra fiata;
   ma i vostri non appreser ben quell'arte."

Allor surse alla vista scoperchiata
   un'ombra lungo questa infino al mento:
   credo che s'era in ginocchie levata.

Dintorno mi guardò, come talento
   avesse di veder s'altri era meco;
   e poi che il sospecciar fu tutto spento,

piangendo disse: "Se per questo cieco
   carcere vai per altezza d'ingegno,
   mio figlio ov'è? perchè non è ei teco?"

Suddenly this sound issued from one of the chests; whereat in fear I drew a little closer to my guide.

And he said to me: "Turn thee round; what art thou doing? lo there Farinata! who has raised himself erect; from the girdle upward thou shalt see him all."

Already I had fixed my look on his; and he rose upright with breast and countenance, as if he entertained great scorn of Hell;

and the bold and ready hands of my Guide pushed me amongst the sepultures to him, saying: "Let thy words be numbered."

When I was at the foot of his tomb he looked at me a little; and then, almost contemptuously, he asked me: "Who were thy ancestors?"

I, being desirous to obey, concealed it not; but opened the whole to him: whereupon he raised his brows a little;

then he said: "Fiercely adverse were they to me, and to my progenitors, and to my party; so that twice I scattered them."

"If they were driven forth, they returned from every quarter, both times," I answered him; "but yours have not rightly learned that art."

Then, beside him, there rose a shadow visible to the chin; it had raised itself, I think, upon its knees.

It looked around me, as if it had a wish to see whether someone were with me; but when all its expectation was quenched,

it said, weeping: "If through this blind prison thou goest through height of genius, where is my son and why is he not with thee?"

61   *E io a lui: "Da me stesso non vegno:*
       colui ch'attende là, per qui mi mena,
       forse cui Guido vostro ebbe a disdegno".

    Le sue parole e 'l modo della pena
       m'avean di costui già letto il nome;
       però fu la risposta così piena.

    Di subito drizzato gridò: "Come
       dicesti? elli ebbe? non viv'elli ancora?
       non fiere li occhi suoi il dolce lome?"

    Quando s'accorse d'alcuna dimora
       ch'io facea dinanzi alla risposta,
       supin ricadde e più non parve fora.

    Ma quell'altro magnanimo a cui posta
       restato m'era, non mutò aspetto,
       nè mosse collo, nè piegò sua costa;

    e sè continuando al primo detto,
       "S'elli han quell'arte" disse "male appresa,
       ciò mi tormenta più che questo letto.

    Ma non cinquanta volte fia raccesa
       la faccia della donna che qui regge,
       che tu saprai quanto quell'arte pesa.

    E se tu mai nel dolce mondo regge,
       dimmi: perchè quel popol è sì empio
       incontr'a'miei in ciascuna sua legge?"

    Ond'io a lui: "Lo strazio e 'l grande scempio
       che fece l'Arbia colorata in rosso,
       tali orazion fa far nel nostro tempio."

    Poi ch'ebbe sospirato e 'l capo scosso,
       "A ciò non fu'io sol" disse, "nè certo
       sanza cagion con li altri sarei mosso.

    Ma fu' io solo, là dove sofferto
       fu per ciascun di torre via Fiorenza,
       colui che la difesi a viso aperto."

And I to him: "Of myself I come not; he, that waits yonder, leads me through this place; whom perhaps thy Guido held in disdain."

Already his words and the manner of his punishment had read his name to me; hence my answer was so full.

Rising instantly erect, he cried: "How saidst thou? He had? lives he not still? does not the sweet light strike his eyes?"

When he perceived that I made some delay in answering, supine he fell again, and showed himself no more.

But that other, magnanimous, at whose desire I had stopped, changed not his aspect, nor moved his neck, nor bent his side.

"And if," continuing his former words, he said, "they have learnt that art badly, it more torments me than this bed.

But the face of the Queen who reigns here, shall not be fifty times rekindled ere thou shalt know the hardness of that art.

And so mayest thou once return to the sweet world, tell me why that people is so fierce against my kindred in all its laws?"

Whereat I to him: "The havoc and the great slaughter which dyed the Arbia red, causes such oration in our temple."

And sighing, he shook his head; then said: "In that I was not single; nor without cause, assuredly, should I have stirred with the others;

but I was single there, where all consented to extirpate Florence, I alone with open face defended her."

94   "Deh, se riposi mai vostra semenza"
        prega'io lui, "solvetemi quel nodo
        che qui ha inviluppata mia sentenza.

    El par che voi veggiate, se ben odo,
        dinanzi quel che 'l tempo seco adduce,
        e nel presente tenete altro modo."

    "Noi veggiam, come quei c'ha mala luce,
        le cose" disse "che ne son lontano;
        cotanto ancor ne splende il sommo duce.

    Quando s'appressano o son, tutto è vano
        nostro intelletto; e s'altri non ci apporta,
        nulla sapem di vostro stato umano.

    Però comprender puoi che tutta morta
        fia nostra conoscenza da quel punto
        che del futuro fia chiusa la porta."

    Allor, come di mia colpa compunto,
        dissi: "Or direte dunque a quel caduto
        che 'l suo nato è co' vivi ancor congiunto;

    e s'i' fui, dianzi, alla risposta muto,
        fate i saper che 'l feci che pensava
        già nell'error che m'avete soluto."

115   E già il maestro mio mi richiamava . . .

"Ah! so may thy seed sometime have rest," I prayed him, "solve the knot which has here involved my judgment.

It seems that you see beforehand what time brings with it, if I rightly hear; and have a different manner with the present."

"Like one who has imperfect vision, we see the things," he said, "which are remote from us; so much light the Supreme Ruler still gives to us;

when they draw nigh, or are, our intellect is altogether
void; and except what others bring us, we know nothing of your human state.

Therefore thou mayest understand that all our knowledge shall be dead from that moment when the portal
of the future shall be closed."

Then, as compunctious for my fault, I said: "Now will
you therefore tell that fallen one, that his child is still
joined to the living.

And if I was mute before, at the response, let him
know it was because my thoughts already were in that
error which you have resolved for me."

And now my Master was recalling me. . . .

X, 22–115

It is almost a standard article of Dante criticism that
this scene shows us a noble patriot who, though still in-
clined to political feuding, rises strongly above the pain
of Hell to talk of his fatherland and father-city with the
child of his enemies; and that it sets him in relief against
the pathetic Cavalcanti, whose wounded paternal love cuts
him off early from the encounter. This approach (matched
by the standard treatment of other scenes in the *Comedy*)
assumes in Dante, the author of the poem, a romantic
preoccupation with individual character and emotion—a
romantic and wholly alien yearning to exonerate the
strayed sheep. This is in part perhaps the result of con-
fusing the clear-sighted, educated Dante who writes the
poem with the ignorant, obedient, diffident and pitiful
protagonist of the fiction. If in every other sort of detail
the poet is concentrated, consequential, integrated in his
poetic rendering of the vision of Hell, and absolutely
austere and unmitigating in his penetration of the nature
and results of the several moral flaws, it would be strange
to find him yielding in his portrait of Farinata. Deviation
into pity—and even more, into admiration for resistance to
the pains of Hell—should be totally foreign to such a mind.

One would expect in Dante's book not only absence of such extraneous expressions of personal concern, on the author's part, but in all sections of the work a continuous bearing out of the themes, major and minor.

Then what, one may enquire, has a discussion of the Florentine Guelph-Ghibelline rivalry got to do with major themes, or with the sin, itself, of heresy? And how does a father's devotion to his son connect with that sin, or with political rivalry?

The questions begin to find an answer as soon as one stops assuming in Dante an orthodoxy of definition to which he never lays claim. Over and over again in the Inferno Dante enlarges and redefines the narrow categories of sin which he has extracted from one or another revered tradition. This he does occasionally in a phrase which the dramatic action later develops (as when in Canto V he speaks of the carnal sinners as those "who subject reason to lust"), but far more often through the dramatic action, the imagery and the diction, alone. Thus the "scenes" in Hell are the true demonstrations of the nature of error. They *are* "experience"—and as such properly contain the clues to all general ideas. This relationship of experience to knowledge Dante shows us frequently in the questions (followed always by answers) which arise out of the protagonist's participation in certain "scenes". But the other face of the coin—the incommensurability of experience and reason—this he gives us by allowing the dramatic interludes to expound what Virgil cannot attempt to word. And so in Canto X, after the small preparatory shock of learning that the pagan Epicurus is numbered among these Heretics, we find in the dramatic encounter a presentation of heresy as not merely breach of Christian faith, and not merely breach of that eternal divine love which proceeds from God as well as toward him, and embraces all mankind—but all failure to see and to maintain the essential unity (political and moral) of the earthly city. This failure occurs when the ego clings to some fraction or splinter of the whole, which it itself has nurtured. Epicurus clung to the splinter, mortal body. And Farinata? Farinata is a political partisan; a partisan soul, which, all deeds being past and done, yet embodies the spirit of faction and divides the city of man.

The dramatic expatiation of this broad view of heresy is bound closely together by two symbols: blindness or short-sightedness (the arch-complaint of all residents of Hell) and isolation (the tomb) which is a consequence of the first.

We see first the pilgrim and Virgil alone on the "wide plain". The covers of the tombs are raised but not a soul is in sight, and the pilgrim enquires whether he may not see those whose sighs he can hear. Then Farinata rises up almost lovingly at the mere sound of the Tuscan language coming from a speaker who must have been invisible to him as he lay within the tomb. (If the tomb is his encasement of spirit, what we see in this response is the positive side of love of country which is able to bring Farinata at least halfway out of his isolation.)

The pilgrim at first sound of Farinata's voice quails, failing to see the speaker and fearing what he cannot see. It is Virgil who turns him round in the right direction, half admonishing him for his mistake in vision and feeling, and then urging him forward. Farinata, on his part, lifts up chest and forehead "as if he entertained great scorn of Hell", waits for the pilgrim to reach his tomb, then asks abruptly and "almost contemptuously" for the names of his forebears. This passage corrects our first impression of the sinner. To scorn Hell when one is in it is to scorn the condition of one's own soul, the source of one's anguish—and is perhaps also to scorn the condition of those other souls which have embraced error. The contemptuous question to the pilgrim gives warning of the clan pride (isolation) which is about to emerge in bitterness and anger when the living man's answer shows him to be a Guelph and son of Guelphs. In the reaction to that answer—in the raising of Farinata's wonderfully expressive brows—we see that the question itself was not directed at making a distinction but at asserting a barrier. The difference is an essential one extremely important to Dante, who gives us a dozen different opportunities to think about it throughout the *Comedy*: we come upon it in the words written above the gates of Hell, in Justinian's statement of the need for diverse talents and offices in the earthly city, in the presence of Sigier of Brabant in Paradise, in Dante's question to Peter Damian.

Farinata's words (lines 46–48) bear out the raising of his brows with the brusque statement of his enmity and his party's triumph over the Guelphs. And this in turn brings the pilgrim full into the bloom of his own capacity for the partisan sin (lines 49–51). His retort crackles.

With lines 52–73 the reader is drawn abruptly into a new phase of the divisive heresy. The shade who rises here from the tomb he shares with Farinata is the father of Dante's friend and fellow-poet, Guido Cavalcanti. Enough has already been written in praise of the pathos, the economy, the surprise, the contrast of the scene to make its deeper purpose sink quite out of sight. But one does not do Dante justice when one overlooks the co-presence of his superhuman judgment with his human sympathy. Cavalcanti's sin is as much a part of this scene as his fatherly love and grief—or, to put it more accurately, his suffering has its source in his sin. Rising part way from his tomb (one must assume he has heard the voyager name himself to Farinata), he looks not at the living man but all around him, searching for his own boy; and he speaks of the dubious honour of a trip through Hell as though it were a fellowship which the authorities should not have withheld from one young poet if they accorded it to his friend. He asks why his Guido is not there, misunderstands the past tense of the pilgrim's answer in an almost wilful way, and falls backward (*supin ricadde*) into his tomb in desperation—not waiting for an answer merely because that answer is a little slow in coming.

At this point occurs a crucial and dramatic return to the figure of Farinata (line 73 ff.), who has not budged during the whole of Cavalcanti's emergence, nor removed his attention from the pilgrim's last rankling retort to him. The textual commentaries continue to read in this picture, these verses, the noble concentration of a soul whose love of country surpasses his suffering of Hell's torment. But such a reading ignores Dante's whole demonstration that the pain of Hell is the pain of sin, itself. What Farinata suffers from, as the scene tells us, is the ache of pride and the anguish of partisanship. These are the flames and the tomb—the unbendingness and the contempt. Like many other occupants of Hell, Farinata does not know he is in it.

And furthermore it is not love of country, but of party, that has animated Farinata in the whole interchange up to this point. What he has waited so steadfastly to say to the pilgrim Guelph is merely this: that the failure of the Ghibellines is torment to him, indeed—but just let young Alighieri wait: he will pay in due time the cost of *his* party's victory.

"But that other, magnanimous . . . changed not his aspect, nor moved his neck, nor bent his side." The figure is a striking one, especially following upon the dreary collapse of Cavalcanti. And *magnanimous* (*magnanimo*) is a handsome epithet. But how are we to take this word? Clearly it cannot signify large-souled generosity, for Farinata has stood stiff-necked, his face concentrated on his interrupted argument all during the sad father's appearance. Totally oblivious to his tomb-mate's sorrow and error (again in blindness[12]), he has waited with grim tolerance for the moment when he could once more take up his own theme. And yet, there is something else in Farinata—an ability to stand up unflinchingly before the pain he brings on himself, a willingness to hear the "enemy" out in full—to which Dante pays its due in the word *magnanimo*.

When the pilgrim has answered Farinata's question (lines 82–84), acknowledging the partisan vengeance of contemporary Florence, the scene enters its final phase. Farinata sighs; and from this point on the tempo and the spirit of the interchange grow pacific. Although no full

[12] Blindness, one might say, with trimmings: for Cavalcanti's son was Farinata's son-in-law, according to history.

recognition in the Aristotelian sense can possibly occur in Hell (which is by nature the place of those who fail to "recognize"), the man and the shade in this scene now see each other for a moment, not as rivals, but as citizens of one dear and much-troubled city; and Farinata recalls to himself and to the voyager the great moment in Tuscan history when his love for Florence outweighed his partisan wrath, and saved the city from razing. The pilgrim questions him on the foresight of the damned, and learns in a literal exposition what the reader knows in its metaphorical extension: that those in Hell are blind to present events in the world. Farinata re-enters his tomb. The pilgrim and Virgil move together again alone on the wide plain. The young man's mind reverts to Farinata's dark and angry words of prophecy; and the canto ends with Virgil's answering reproof: remember what you've heard, but put your mind on the final goal of your journey. He admonishes all partisans.

The dramatic action of this canto of Heretics is, then, the dogged clinging to one's own clan, one's own side, with consequent failure to see humanity whole and to live in it accordingly. The "other" man is either an opponent (as the pilgrim is in Farinata's view) or else quite imperceptible (as Cavalcanti is in Farinata's view); the sense either of injury received or triumph experienced obscures sympathy and undoes the soul's equilibrium. The sin of Farinata is linked by this action with that of Epicurus, who divides the wholeness of life by disregarding the soul's immortality, and with that of the Christian heretic, who divides the earthly church. The image of Farinata and Cavalcanti, shut eternally in a single tomb, suffering the same flames, yet unaware of one another, stands for the whole concept of divisiveness. And the circle of the isolated Heretics, inside the walls of the City of Dis, but above and distinct from the circles of the Violent and the Fraudulent, forms along with these other two a graduated trio of those modes of action by which man, in Dante's *Comedy*, digs himself deliberately into the dark.

(c) PIER DELLA VIGNA

Inferno, Canto XIII

The meeting between the pilgrim and the suicide, Pier della Vigna, takes place in a notable wood, a pathless circle of hideous trees and shrubs, lying between the circular river of blood, Phlegethon, and the fiery sands of the Sodomites.

> *Non fronda verde, ma di color fosco;*
> *non rami schietti, ma nodosi e 'nvolti;*
> *non pomi v'eran, ma stecchi con tosco.*

Not green the foliage, but of colour dusky; not smooth the branches, but gnarled and warped; apples none were there, but withered sticks with poison.

XIII, 4–6

On these unnatural trees sit the big-bellied harpies, eating the dark leaves with their human mouths. The only sound one hears at first is their lament. Then there is another wailing, from all sides, but no visible wailers. The pilgrim is bewildered and at cross-purposes. Virgil, although he knows both what the situation is and his companion's puzzlement, does not explain the incredible fact that these trees are souls, but directs the pilgrim to break off a small branch from one of them.

31　　*Allor porsi la mano un poco avante,*
> *e colsi un ramicel da un gran pruno;*
> *e 'l tronco suo gridò: "Perchè mi schiante?"*

> *Da che fatto fu poi di sangue bruno,*
> *ricominciò a dir: "Perchè mi scerpi?*
> *non hai tu spirto di pietà alcuno?*

> *Uomini fummo, e or siam fatti sterpi:*
> *ben dovrebb'esser la tua man più pia,*
> *se state fossimo anime di serpi."*

40 Come d'un stizzo verde ch'arso sia
    dall'un de' capi, che dall'altro geme
    e cigola per vento che va via,

sì della schieggia rotta usciva inseme
    parole e sangue; ond'io lasciai la cima
    cadere, e stetti come l'uom che teme.

"S'elli avesse potuto creder prima"
    rispuose 'l savio mio, "anima lesa,
    ciò c'ha veduto pur con la mia rima,

non averebbe in te la man distesa;
    ma la cosa incredibile mi fece
    indurlo ad ovra ch'a me stesso pesa.

Ma dilli chi tu fosti, sì che 'n vece
    d'alcun ammenda tua fama rinfreschi
    nel mondo su, dove tornar li lece."

E 'l tronco: "Sì col dolce dir m'adeschi
    ch' i' non posso tacere; e voi non gravi
    perch' io un poco a ragionar m'inveschi.

Io son colui che tenni ambo le chiavi
    del cor di Federigo, e che le volsi,
    serrando e diserrando, sì soavi,

che dal secreto suo quasi ogn'uom tolsi:
    fede portai al glorioso offizio,
    tanto ch' i' ne perde' li sonni e' polsi.

La meretrice che mai dall'ospizio
    di Cesare non torse li occhi putti,
    morte comune, delle corti vizio,

infiammò contra me li animi tutti;
    e li 'nfiammati infiammar sì Augusto,
    che' lieti onor tornaro in tristi lutti.

L'animo mio, per disdegnoso gusto,
    credendo col morir fuggir disdegno,
    ingiusto fece me contra me giusto.

73   *Per le nove radici d'esto legno*
      vi giuro che già mai non ruppi fede
      al mio signor, che fu d'onor sì degno.

      E se di voi alcun nel mondo riede,
      conforti la memoria mia, che giace
78   *ancor del colpo che 'nvidia le diede."*

Then I stretched my hand a little forward, and plucked a branchlet from a great thorn; and the trunk of it cried, "Why dost thou rend me?"

And when it had grown dark with blood, it again began to cry: "Why dost thou tear me? Hast thou no breath of pity?

Men we were, and now are turned to trees: truly thy hand should be more merciful, had we been souls of serpents."

As a green brand, that is burning at one end, at the other drops, and hisses with the wind which is escaping:

so from the broken splint, words and blood came forth together: whereat I let fall the top, and stood like one who is afraid.

"If he, O wounded Spirit!" my sage replied, "could have believed before what he has seen only in my verse,

he would not have stretched forth his hand against thee; but the incredibility of the thing made me prompt him to do what grieves myself.

But tell him who thou wast; so that to make thee some amends, he may refresh thy fame up in the world, to which he is permitted to return."

And the trunk: "Thou so allurest me with thy sweet words that I cannot keep silent; and let it not seem burdensome to you if I enlarge a little in discourse.

I am he who held both keys of Frederick's heart, and
turned them locking and unlocking so softly,

that from his secrets I excluded almost every other
man; so great fidelity I bore to the glorious office, that
I lost thereby both sleep and life.

The harlot, that never from Caesar's dwelling turned
her adulterous eyes, common bane, and vice of courts,

inflamed all minds against me; and these, being inflamed, so inflamed Augustus, that my joyous honours were changed to dismal sorrows.

My soul, in its disdainful mood, thinking to escape
disdain by death, made me, though just, unjust
against myself.

By the new roots of this tree, I swear to you, never
did I break faith to my lord, who was so worthy of
honour.

And if any of you return to the world, strengthen the
memory of me, which still lies prostrate from the
blow that envy gave it."

XIII, 31–78

Here, as in the two cantos just discussed, Dante has
conceived the torment as an image of the particular sin
in its controlling and shaping of souls which have yielded
to it; while in the dramatic image—the scene between individual sinner and pilgrim—he has both extended the
conventional definition of the sin and explored its psychological groundwork.

Souls transformed into wizened shrubs—what do they
signify? We see that they are immobilized souls, bound
under a seemingly insentient disguise. This is not difficult
to understand; yet we are apt to oversimplify our reading
of it if we assume that self-inflicted bodily death is what
the poet refers to. Cato of Utica, who killed himself in
order not to fall into Caesar's enemy hands, is not in Hell
at all, but posted with much honour as guardian of the

entry to Purgatory. Dido and Cleopatra are blown by the winds of the second Circle. Dante does not define this or any other sin according to the technicality of a material act, but, as his *Paradiso* teaches, measures all things according to their essences. Thus he plants here among the Violent-against-themselves, souls which have followed out to its ultimate consequences a given *disposition* rather than shared a given deed. His anguished trees represent an attitude of blindness and violence of soul, not so much towards body as towards the role in which the Soul finds itself cast. Bodily suicide may or may not follow; it is in any case merely symptomatic.[13]

Cato, when he killed himself, did so in defence of what he considered a dominant principle within the framework of life itself: namely, liberty. Thus he relinquished his life affirmatively; he did not attack it. The stunted, soul-infested grove of the seventh Circle suggests a wholly different impulse: a denial and rejection. Its souls have balked at their whole human role, because the terms have grown unpleasant or painful. They are thus related to the sulkers (the *accidiosi*), who also hide out from life under their bubbling mud, but who fall short of violence.

But whether the suicidal soul chooses the literal death of its body or some living disguise, in order to be out of reach of what distresses it, it cannot destroy the living principle of its identity which, according to the Christian view is, *ipso facto*, eternal; thus it cannot free itself of what offends it except by ridding itself of its preoccupation with offence—which is to say, of its sin. The true suicide, whom we see in Dante's circle of thorny trees, is entirely possessed by his negative concern, his desire not to be victimized, not to be "there" any more at all, not to

---

13 It is well to remember here that this round of Hell, like every other, extends its reference to sinners above ground. According to Dante's metaphoric conception, the world is full of dead souls in apparent health—persons in whom, as he says in a passage of the *Convivio*, "the man is dead, but the beast survives". The Inferno is a selective mirror of the world; it stands to reason that if suicides are part of it they must be suicides before as well as after they cut their throats or hang themselves.

be in the game. He suffers a more limited and limiting concentration of the will than anything Hell has shown us so far in seven circles.

The tree image makes this all palpable by being, as it were, the prison-shape of escape, the rigid, barren representation of rejection. And the wounded briar gives proof that both vulnerability and pain are more horrible when the will is thus rigidified and concentrated. It would appear that each soul in this forest has achieved the retreat from life at the cost of permanent devotion to its negative role: it must work at being a tree from the moment its seed is scattered (lines 94–103); it must take root wherever the seed falls, grow up in gnarled branches and put out its painful leaves. It must act the part of bramble or tree without ever achieving proper tree-ness or self-forgetfulness. And it must suffer the wounding and pain that may be inflicted even by an innocent passer-by, since it has itself chosen to deny its identity. Nor does it escape its private anguish: the Harpies are with it always. Its species is for the most part thorn or bramble, unpleasant to the touch. Dostoevsky's Underground Man is such a suicide, nursing his angry self-consciousness, watching for slights and insults, miserable in his withdrawal, and false and violent in his forays upon life. And Hamlet, meditating his offences, delaying action, always more preoccupied with his own image than with any other, has the germ in him.

In order to see what the dramatic image of the canto adds to this, one does best to return again to the beginning of the canto, the setting of the scene and the sensuous and emotional tone. Lines 4–6 in the original text bite into the ear as well as the eye with their three smooth, sweet-sounding negations, each followed immediately by an ugly and sibilant affirmation of the dark, twisted, unnatural scene: "di color fosco" . . . "ma nodosi e 'nvolti" . . . "ma stecchi con tosco". The harshness and difficulty of these lines is followed by a split second of relief, as the eye is made to range backward for a glance at the world, in which we see the contrary of all this unnatural vegetation: cultivated Italian fields, the town of Corneto and its river.

A different sort of memory is differently evoked a moment later. When Aeneas and his companions landed in the Strophades, the hateful Harpies would not let them eat their meal in peace, but flew above them and defiled their food. We are supposed to remember this, and to be alerted for malice from them, here, too. It is their chewing of the poison-bearing leaves that makes the wretched trees lament. They "give pain, and to pain an outlet". So perverse, in fact, is this whole forest that even the poet's thought in returning to it becomes twisted and involved: "I think he thought that I was thinking . . ." he says, guessing redundantly at Virgil's interpretation of his bewilderment.

Virgil has of course clearly read his pupil's puzzlement. Wanting him to have an answer in experience rather than words, he tells him to break off a branch from any of the trees. With the breaking of the branch the tree cries out in protest no less than pain: "Why dost thou rend me?" It knows perfectly well that it appears to be a tree, and the breaking was done in innocence; and yet it rebukes: "thy hand should be more merciful had we been souls of serpents". This is the first hint we get that it is an *anima lesa*—an *offended* soul.

The pilgrim, seeing the blood and hearing the words pour from the broken stump, lets fall the branch he holds and drops back to stand "like one who is afraid", speechless. Virgil steps in as it were to cover this silence; he explains his own responsibility for the breaking, makes his apology, and gently coaxes the soul to tell its story.

From here on Dante's art in the little scene is characteristic. He has, in the first place, chosen as his principal tree-soul an Italian statesman and poet of much celebrity, not long dead, whose actual story is perfectly adapted to the psychological content he has in mind. This means he can count on his contemporary readers' sense of Piero's reality to enhance the dramatic interest of his own characterization, while at the same time he moulds his presen-

tation with the utmost subtlety to reveal the secret colouring of the sin. There is not a single obvious touch to this
moulding: nothing in Piero's speech appears to point at
all to a moral flaw. On the contrary: the surface of his
speech hides his sin from us as from himself. Yet when
we listen intently to him we see that the self-consciousness
and rigid personal pride of the man are what have led
him to this wooden stultification; and they are Dante's
prime ingredients of suicide.

When Virgil has spoken his apology, the angry suicide
answers, entirely soothed. "Thou so allurest me with thy
sweet words that I cannot keep silent," he replies, and all
his earlier brusqueness disappears in easy graciousness.
There is pure courtliness in this, for he clears Virgil of any
obligation to him for what he is about to tell, pretending
that it is he, Piero, who begs the patience of a listening
ear. But there is also a real desire to hold the stage for a
while before two eager listeners. And he begins his story
in a phrase of large and prideful ease that sets the whole
tonality of his character: "Io son colui che tenni ambo le
chiavi / del cor di Federigo . . ." ("I am he who held both
the keys of Frederick's heart . . .")

Who else in all Inferno thinks of himself in so ringing a
third person, in an "I am he"? Not Mahomet nor Pope
Anastasius nor Ulysses. No one (except possibly Farinata,
who does not need to introduce himself) has such a sense
of magnificence resulting from his earthly role.[14] Piero
seems to have no inkling of the ironic fatuity of his *I am he*
as it issues from a broken branch in Hell, and he proceeds with his story, couching all of it in high language
that befits his former role and survives in his conception
of the "glorious office" and his "happy honours". He sets
store by his acknowledgment that he served the emperor
without rest, that he shut other men out of the mon-
arch's confidence, that his success was food for envy. Even

---

[14] Outside the *Comedy* there is of course Walt Whitman, whose
"I am he that aches with amorous love," caused D. H. Lawrence
to write certain deathless pages of hilarious rebuke in his *Studies
in Classic American Literature.*

when he speaks of his downfall, self-consciousness inflates
his style and rhetorical conceits take precedence over feeling. Envy is the "harlot" who "inflamed all minds against
me" so that "these, being inflamed . . . inflamed Augustus". His spirit "in its disdainful mood, thinking to escape
disdain by death", led him to his suicide, "though just,
unjust against myself". These phrases are tailored to measure for Piero by a poet who on his own part regarded fine
writing as the opposite of inflated rhetoric: a scrupulous
correspondence of language to thought and feeling.

Only when Piero has finished his narrative, and come
to his plea that someone refresh his memory in the living
world, does feeling break through the ornate style to word
a simple and pathetic entreaty. And, although it is still his
reputation that concerns Piero, what he asks now is not
that it be adorned, but relieved of its undeserved stain.

Let us not be misled by the fact that the historical Piero
was a courtier (and no doubt a skilled and refined one)
into assuming that anything in the portrait Dante gives
of him is there with the purpose of illustrating history.
Piero della Vigna was chancellor to Frederick the Second
of Sicily. Esteemed in his official function, he was also
praised as a writer of verse in the troubadour style, and
of Latin prose. He is said to have committed suicide in
despair when imprisoned by Frederick under a false accusation of treachery. Commentators who treat the great
figures of the *Comedy* as independent displays of Dante's
skill in portraiture have pointed out the historic verisimili-
tude of Piero's language in the *Inferno*. And it is true that
the antitheses, the metaphors and conceits of his speech
suggest the conventionalized ornate style of the provençal-
izing poet and courtier—perhaps also that of the Latin es-
sayist. But Dante in his *Comedy* never *serves* history; he
uses it, as I have suggested, by extracting from it such
characters and traits as suit his primary purpose by lending
the depth of another sort of reality to the fiction.

The fiction remains paramount. Its purpose in Piero's
case—as in Francesca's and Farinata's—is to show us, in a
framework that shall seem as real as possible, the opera-

tion of the moral flaw that deforms the soul, twisting even
its virtues to its undoing. The purpose is very large and
the space for its execution relatively small. There is no
room for either "history" or emotion which is not also in
the service of the true theme. Thus, to have noticed that
Piero's style is historically correct is scarcely to do Dante
honour enough. One must at least ask how, in addition, it
suits the portraiture of suicide.

To begin with, such a delight in artifice would, under
any circumstances, suggest a dangerous shying away from
the simple line of truth. But Piero's circumstances are not
ordinary. His public life has been destroyed, the confidence of an emperor snatched from him unjustly. One
would expect even an orator to retract his oratorical style
on such a subject; yet Piero wraps his memory of these
things in florid ornament. As Francesco De Sanctis has
pointed out, not even the supreme moment of his death
wakens any real memory in him; it issues from his lips
as a conceit.[15] Speech of this sort suggests an intense and
rigid consciousness of role. Indeed, so alive is he to "form"
and "face" that not even his present shape and theatre can
deflate him. The figure he cuts is, as it was in his life, the
first object of his concern. He will no more part with
his elegance of rhetoric than he would, when the circumstances required it of him, exchange his elegant position
for a humbled one. Thus his speech shows exactly what
his death did: the rigid "suicidal" refusal to bend to the
reality of change. Because he saw and felt grandiloquently
about himself in Frederick's court, caring for his elevation rather than the excellent qualities which had brought
him to it, he rushed headlong out of life as soon as the
world punctured his glory. Which is to say he rushed into
a stunted and vegetative brooding—clinging to his ornate
memories, and with his anachronistic funeral oration ever
at his lips.

The position is individual, but not unique; for Dante is
pointing out in Piero both the ultimate deadliness and the
egocentric cause of all inability to face life when the terms

[15] F. De Sanctis, *op. cit.*, p. 259

of fortune run counter to desire; and he is issuing a warning with regard to the lesser degrees of "suicide" that are involved in every clinging to the forms of a role when the role has been cancelled.

The theme of Piero's death would appear to end in the thirteenth canto; but as is very frequently the case with infernal themes in the echoing-chamber of the *Comedy*, it is called to mind again with quiet insistence by a figure in the *Paradiso*. Romeo di Villanova, who thrives in the heaven of Mercury among the Honour-seeking, is Piero's exact counterpart with respect to Fortune's dealings. We are told that he had been steward to Count Raymond Berengar, for many years honoured and rewarded with high confidence, but at length brought under suspicion of thievery by the slander of jealous enemies. He had answered his accusation by demonstrating that he had increased rather than despoiled his lord's fortunes. Then he had gone his way, alone and empty-handed. "And might the world know the heart he had within him, begging his life crust by crust, much as it praiseth, it would praise him more."[16]

I do not see how it would be possible to doubt that Dante had Piero in mind when he wrote this passage and gave this momentary reminder that a man reduced by slander may conclude in bliss. No doubt, too, it gave Dante a sly pleasure to show this courageous and flexible soul not only blessed, not merely spoken for in Heaven by an emperor, but, as the last line indicates, possessed of the very trifle poor Piero coveted: the world's praises.

But the wisdom which a traveller may gather in the heaven of Mercury is absent in Hell, and Dante's pilgrim, lacking it, can only listen to Piero in fear and silence. The reader may have remarked this silence which makes the meeting with the suicides so different from those with Farinata and Francesca. One might think here that Dante, intent on the dramatic monologue primarily, had cast Virgil and the pilgrim as mere prompters. Yet not quite. The pilgrim's silence is far from empty, although attention

16 *Par.* VI, 140–142

centres on him only twice, very briefly, during the whole encounter. When at the beginning he breaks the branch and hears it cry out, red with blood, "Why dost thou rend me?" he drops the part he holds, and stands back "like one who is afraid". That spare affirmation suggests a quick response of horror—the hand opening of itself to let fall what now must seem virtually a human limb torn from its body. If the suggestion is intended, the pilgrim's silence is filled up with intentness rather than indifference. And this is borne out a little later by his reply to Virgil's suggestion that he question Piero further, on the way in which the souls grow up into their vegetable forms. "Do thou ask him . . ." the pilgrim says, "for I could not, such pity is upon my heart."[17]

Fear and pity—both haunt the pilgrim throughout the circles of the Incontinent and the Violent, and suggest always in this living traveller, who is at once himself and every man, some potentiality for the sin in question. Thus it is tempting to read into his present tongue-tied withdrawal some trace of Piero's own malady. This would not be without foundation; for one of the factual themes that flows from Dante's own life into his fictional hero is that of his exile from Florence at the beginning of a more than promising career in politics and letters. The exile lies behind the *Comedy's* author and ahead of its pilgrim hero; it is foreshadowed time and time again in the text, darkly and bitterly at first, but each time with more light, until the moral preparation for the actual fact is complete. Farinata had begun the chain of foreboding hints, warning the pilgrim that within fifty moons he too would learn the difficulties of the road home from banishment. This news the pilgrim took so broodingly that Virgil had, later, to call him back out of his "bewilderment", cautioning him against the folly of drawing conclusions from incomplete knowledge. Does he now stand before Piero listening to the quailing of his own heart in a brotherhood of feeling, and equal readiness to turn his back angrily on life if Fortune mishandles him? It is a conjecture, certainly; but

[17] XIII, 82–84

a conjecture that seems borne out in the canto following the present meeting when a fresh allusion to the troubles in store for him brings a totally reverse response. To Brunetto Latini's warnings he says: "I am prepared for Fortune as she wills," with such evident bravado that he draws an odd, wry look from sober Virgil.

Pity and fear colour all three of the cantos we have discussed. Pity in so far as each of them recognizes the easy bent of the human soul towards its immediate delight, and the easy, almost innocent closing of its eyes to the losses it may incur by yielding. But fear, too, in so far as each recognizes the sternness with which the error damns. Shivering, ignorant as he is, the pilgrim, seeking to understand divine justice, does not dissent from it in his pity. He stands before it in tears because he glimpses—half glimpses but cannot yet seize—the inescapable "reason" of the damning justice, together with the frailty of the justiced. He stands before it in pity and awe, learning what sorts of love beget what sorts of pain, and dimly groping towards some understanding of why there should be pain at all.

Implications of an answer stir faintly under the cover of the intense experiences he undergoes. It is quite possible that he already sees the wonderful likeness between each infernal suffering and its sin. It is possible that he knows that divine justice does not retaliate for evil. Hell is a vast hall of objective correlatives, matching the inner dispositions of its souls; and the pain it offers is the pain each sinner has brought with him. But, it may be asked, if his disposition has not brought its horrid consequences during his lifetime in the world, why then pain at all? Why is the Heretic not happy in his superior philosophy; why should the successful Barrator not revel forever on the income of his graft; what makes the Flatterer, Thais, do anything but enjoy her treasures? The answer is implicit in the imagery of the *Inferno* and confirmed by the wisdom of the *Purgatorio*: that the idea of the soul's good modelled on the absolute Good, is written as firmly into the soul's being from its beginning as the oak-tree goal is in any acorn. Loosed into the world, open to a thousand desires, it is at liberty to follow any lures it chooses, but never to free itself from the "good" norm. Either it copies that model or else it suffers. Every lapse is bound to pain it; and not because the authorities are watching, not in retaliation, but because *as* lapse it goes against the grain of the soul.

This essential principle the reader sees as soon as he looks beyond the physical pains of Hell (whose burns and lacerations have, after all, nothing but shadows to gall), and grasps that its various flames and whips are themselves only representations of the soul's desires in action. They can hurt only as they deform the soul with respect to the good that it cannot possibly refrain from loving.

Thus the Carnal Lovers suffer, not because the winds of passion are themselves more painful than the bolts of reason, but because by their given nature they covet rational self-mastery; the Heretics grieve in their burning isolation because the soul of its own accord always seeks harmony and wholeness; the Suicides are pained by the disguises they have themselves selected, because an open striving between soul and world is the only basis for the free, living growth they cannot keep from loving.

Any sinner who recognizes in time the true cause of his suffering makes, by this very fact, the choice of Purgatory.

Chapter III

FOUR IMAGES OF
FRATERNAL LOVE

*Wise people after they have listened to the laws, be-
come serene: like a deep, smooth and still lake.*
THE BUDDHA

There are four scenes in the *Purgatorio* which are so closely
linked by internal developments as well as by external
form, and each so reinforced and augmented by its relationships with the others, that it would be difficult to know
any one of them well without seeing it in its role as a part
of the series—and impossible to consider the series without experiencing it as *one* thing, somewhat greater than
the sum of its parts. I select these for discussion here because, individually and as a group, they give a fresh clue
to the quality and meaning of Dante's poetry in this second book of the *Comedy*. They show something of its
limpid tranquillity, its rational framework, its view of art
as an instrument of human excellence; and they show the
unity and growth of the mountain journey which forms
the second stage of the pilgrim's education.

Each of these scenes is a meeting between either Virgil
or the pilgrim and the shade of some fellow-craftsman
(three are poets, one a minstrel) with whom he is linked
by a special tie of sympathy. Each defines a condition of
the soul through an image of action which is repeated,
with significant variations, as the travellers move upward

on the "mount where reason probes us". In every case there is an encounter, an astonished recognition, and an impulse of love that moves at least one of the participants to embrace the other. No meetings in the *Inferno* so closely resemble one another. That is because Inferno is the place of isolation, of the cultivated ego, while Purgatory unites all wills in a common goal, attainable at many different gaits.

What these four meetings express is, first of all, four aspects of love—love in which either no flaw ever existed, or none now survives; fraternal love, transcending all material claims and progressively purified of personal limitation as the series advances. And all of them affirm positively the uncorruptible beauty of things made by man's imagination—things so gracious that the soul can momentarily forget heaven in contemplation of them, solace the journey with talk of them, or, while burning in penitential fire, defend them. These four scenes reveal as a group what Purgatory as a whole reveals: the laboriousness of the way to heaven and the joys that are in both the labour and the journey. This is their noble task, assumed with the full compliance of the poet's belief. And yet, with all their austerity, they express also (with, one guesses, the full compliance of the poet's feeling) pity for the strength and endurance of human attachment to the concrete forms of mortal experience, surviving until the last arduous lesson in detachment is learned.

The meanings that these meetings reveal are at least as clear to the characters as they are to the reader, for darkness of mind ended in Inferno, and everyone in Purgatory knows who he is and why he is here.

FIRST MEETING: CASELLA

The first of the four scenes occurs in Canto II, shortly after the pilgrim's arrival with Virgil at the base of the purgatorial mountain, and immediately after his ritual cleansing in the waters that lap the base of the hill.

The journey begun here and ending in the Terrestrial

Paradise from which Adam fell is the spirit's voluntary climb from its Adam-damaged condition of uneducated awareness of good and evil, to knowledge of all the modes of evil and knowledge and assimilation of all their opposing goods. To begin this journey at all, the soul must be innocent—not as children are innocent, but in the manner of those who have renounced evil. One cannot renounce what one does not know; infants who died sinless do not reach this shore, while Buonconte di Montefeltro, who repented many sins in the hour of his death, is a sure beginner here; and the living pilgrim who has studied Hell and escaped from it may make the difficult climb. Those who come are cleansed (the dead by their repentance, the pilgrim by the waters with which Virgil washed Hell's stains from him) of every desire that pride, greed and lust might motivate. Their baggage is slight: virtually uncritical memory and virtually uninformed faith, hope and charity; but they are free from evil and they desire the good. This is their newness.

Newness and freshness and light fill the scene that Dante sets. Dawn is verging towards morning in Purgatory (Aurora's cheeks are aging); Virgil and the pilgrim are walking along the sea-front "which never saw man navigate its waters who afterward had experience of return", longing to be on their road, but ignorant how to begin:

10   *Noi eravamo lunghesso mare ancora,*
        come gente che pensa a suo cammino,
        che va col cuore e col corpo dimora.

      Ed ecco qual, sul presso del mattino,
        per li grossi vapor Marte rosseggia
        giù nel ponente sovra 'l suol marino,

      cotal m'apparve, s'io ancor lo veggia,
        un lume per lo mar venir sì ratto,
        che 'l mover suo nessun volar pareggia.

      Dal qual com'io un poco ebbi ritratto
        l'occhio per domandar lo duca mio,
        rividil più lucente e maggior fatto.

22   Poi d'ogne lato ad esso m'apparìo
       un, non sapea che, bianco, e di sotto
       a poco a poco un altro a lui uscìo.

     Lo mio maestro ancor non fece motto,
       mentre che i primi bianchi apparser ali:
       allor che ben conobbe il galeotto,

     gridò, "Fa, fa che le ginocchia cali:
       ecco l'angel di Dio: piega le mani:
       omai vedrai di sì fatti officiali.

     Vedi che sdegna gli argomenti umani,
       sì che remo non vuol nè altro velo
       che l'ali sue tra liti sì lontani.

     Vedi come l'ha dritte verso il cielo,
       trattando l'aere con l'etterne penne,
       che non si mutan come mortal pelo."

     Poi, come più e più verso noi venne
       l'uccel divino, più chiaro appariva;
       per che l'occhio da presso nol sostenne,

     ma chinail giuso; e quei sen venne a riva
       con un vasello snelletto e leggiero,
       tanto che l'acqua nulla ne 'nghiottiva.

     Da poppa stava il celestial nocchiero,
       tal che parea beato per iscripto;
       e più di cento spirti entro sediero.

     "In exitu Israel de Aegypto"
       cantavan tutti insieme ad una voce
       con quanto di quel salmo è poscia scripto.

     Poi fece il segno lor di santa croce;
       ond'ei si gittar tutti in su la piaggia:
       ed el sen gì, come venne, veloce.

     La turba che rimase lì, selvaggia
       parea del loco, rimirando intorno
       come colui che nove cose assaggia.

55 *Da tutte parti saettava il giorno*
 lo sol, ch'avea con le saette conte
 di mezzo il ciel cacciato Capricorno,

 quando la nova gente alzò la fronte
 ver noi, dicendo a noi: "Se voi sapete,
 mostratene la via di gire al monte."

 E Virgilio rispuose: "Voi credete
 forse che siamo esperti d'esto loco;
 ma noi siam peregrin come voi siete.

 Dianzi venimmo, innanzi a voi un poco,
 per altra via, che fu sì aspra e forte,
66 *che lo salire omai ne parrà gioco."*

We were alongside the ocean, yet like folk who ponder o'er their road, who in heart do go and in body stay;

and lo, as on the approach of morn, through the dense mists Mars burns red, low in the West o'er the ocean floor;

such to me appeared—so may I see it again!—a light coming o'er the sea so swiftly that no flight is equal to its motion;

from which, when I had a while withdrawn mine eyes to question my Leader, I saw it brighter and bigger grown.

Then on each side of it appeared to me a something white; and from beneath it, little by little, another whiteness came forth.

My Master yet did speak no word, until the first whitenesses appeared as wings; then, when he well knew the pilot,

he cried: "Bend, bend thy knees; behold the Angel of God: fold thy hands: henceforth shalt thou see such ministers.

Look how he scorns all human instruments, so that oar he wills not, nor other sail than his wings, between shores so distant.

See how he has them heavenward turned, plying the air with eternal plumes, that are not mewed like mortal hair."

Then as more and more towards us came the bird divine, brighter yet he appeared, wherefore mine eye endured him not near:

but I bent it down, and he came on to the shore with a vessel so swift and light that the waters nowise drew it in.

On the stern stood the celestial pilot, such, that blessedness seemed writ upon him, and more than a hundred spirits sat within.

"*In exitu Israel de Aegypto*," sang they all together with one voice, with what of that psalm is thereafter written.

Then made he to them the sign of Holy Cross, whereat they all flung them on the strand and quick even as he came he went his way.

The throng that remained there seemed strange to the place, gazing around like one who assayeth new things.

On every side the sun, who with his arrows bright had chased the Goat from midst of heaven, was shooting forth the day,

when the new people lifted up their faces towards us, saying to us: "If ye know show us the way to go to the mount."

And Virgil answered: "Ye think perchance that we have experience of this place, but we are strangers even as ye are.

We came but now, a little while before you, by other
way which was so rough and hard, that the climbing
now will seem but play to us."

II, 10–66

The atmosphere is grave and joyous; the sparkling of the
sun "who with his arrows bright had chased the Goat",
the hymn of release from captivity, the white wings of the
bird divine, and the repetition of the word "new" ("new
things", "new people") converge in an effect of purity and
glad wonder which makes one think sometimes of the landscapes in which Giotto sees St Francis, and sometimes of
Homer's sunlit encounters between gods and men.

The pilgrim's pondering gives way before his astonishment and reverence at the appearance of the angel-skiff.
Momentarily skiff and pilot are the focus of all attention,
filling the immediate scene with whiteness, brightness and
swift fluid motion. But Virgil's phrase, "oar he wills not,
nor other sail than his wings, between shores so distant",
in an instant opens out the visible background of the sea
into the invisible: the reader recalls that this skiff has
crossed the distance from the inhabited world (penitent
souls are gathered up for this journey at the Tiber's
mouth) to the foot of Purgatory; and "see how he holds
them straight towards heaven", spoken of the wings that
have now sailed full into our view, enlarges the scope of
the eye for the briefest moment, sending it backward to
the world and forward to Paradise.

Breadth of view, the natural light, the pagan gods of
natural light, the angelic whiteness, the wings, the song,
and now the gentle crowding and wondering of the new
souls—all these absolute novelties soothe Hell away and
set the tone of a *beginning*—a new journey, a fresh re-
solve. We are in a place of pause, before the burden of
past sin which each soul bears is carried on the first uphill
step of the journey that is to disperse it.

The action of the scene begins when the souls approach
Virgil and the pilgrim to ask their way—and, if one is to
believe the text, *all* lift up their faces and put the question.

(We note it because there were no such concerted gestures
of souls in Hell.) Virgil explains why he cannot answer:
he and his pupil are also pilgrims here, and new ones. At
this point the souls take note that the younger pilgrim
breathes. Pale with wonder, they come closer to stare,
"well nigh forgetting to go and make them fair".[1] One
soul separates itself from the group, and immediately the
reader's eye, which a moment ago was filled with celestial
wings and distant horizons, is held in the narrow focus of
a human event:

> Io vidi una di lor trarresi avante
>   per abbracciarmi, con sì grande affetto,
>   ohe mosse me a fare il simigliante.
>
> Oi ombre vane, fuor che nell'aspetto!
>   Tre volte dietro a lei le mani avvinsi,
>   e tante mi tornai con esse al petto.
>
> Di maraviglia, credo, mi dipinsi;
>   per che l'ombra sorrise e si ritrasse,
>   e io, seguendo lei, oltre mi pinsi.
>
> Soavemente disse ch'io posasse:
>   allor conobbi chi era, e pregai
>   che, per parlarmi, un poco s'arrestasse.
>
> Rispuosemi: "Così com'io t'amai
>   nel mortal corpo, così t'amo sciolta:
>   però m'arresto; ma tu perchè vai?"
>
> "Casella mio, per tornar altra volta
>   là dov'io son, fo io questo viaggio"
>   diss'io; "ma a te com'è tanta ora tolta?"

I saw one of them draw forward to embrace me with
such great affection, that he moved me to do the like.

[1] This is a first hint of a recurrent minor motif of Purgatory:
whoever stops to talk with the living pilgrim (and none refuses)
deliberately gives up something which is precious to him, and
shows thereby the value he sets on human life. On virtually every
terrace of the mountain this common marvelling of souls occurs,
and this homage to the living man. The theme is elaborated in
the scene here to be discussed.

O shades empty save in outward show! thrice behind it my hands I clasped, and as often returned with them to my breast.

With wonder methinks I coloured me, whereat the shade smiled and drew back, and I, following it, flung me forward.

Gently it bade me pause: then knew I who it was, and did pray him that he would stay a while to speak to me.

He answered me: "Even as I loved thee in the mortal body, so do I love thee freed; therefore I stay: but wherefore goest thou?"

"Casella mine, to return here once again where I am, make I this journey," said I, "but how hath so much time been taken from thee?"

Purg. II, 76–93

Casella answers that it is according to God's will that he has waited so long since his death for passage to Purgatory; and the scene continues:

E io: "Se nuova legge non ti toglie
    memoria o uso all'amoroso canto
    che mi solea quetar tutte mie voglie,

di ciò ti piaccia consolare alquanto
    l'anima mia che, con la mia persona,
    venendo qui, è affannata tanto!"

'Amor che nella mente mi ragiona'
    cominciò elli allor sì dolcemente,
    che la dolcezza ancor dentro mi sona.

Lo mio maestro e io e quella gente
    ch'eran con lui parevan sì contenti,
    come a nessun toccasse altro la mente.

Noi eravam tutti fissi e attenti
    alle sue note; ed ecco il veglio onesto
    gridando: "Che è ciò, spiriti lenti?

> *qual negligenza, quale stare è questo?*
> *Correte al monte a spogliarvi lo scoglio*
> *ch'esser non lascia a voi Dio manifesto."*
>
> *Come quando, cogliendo biada o loglio,*
> *li colombi adunati alla pastura,*
> *queti, sanza mostrar l'usato orgoglio,*
>
> *se cosa appare ond'elli abbian paura,*
> *subitamente lasciano star l'esca,*
> *perch'assaliti son da maggior cura;*
>
> *così vid'io quella masnada fresca*
> *lasciar lo canto, e gire inver la costa,*
> *com'uom che va, nè sa dove riesca,*
>
> *nè la nostra partita fu men tosta.*

And I: "If a new law take not from thee memory or skill in that song of love which was wont to calm my every desire,

may it please thee therewith to solace awhile my soul, that, with its mortal form journeying here, is sore distressed."

"*Love that in my mind discourseth to me,*" began he then so sweetly, that the sweetness yet within me sounds.

My Master, and I and that people who were with him, seemed so glad as if to aught else the mind of no one of them gave heed.

We were all fixed and intent upon his notes; and lo the old man venerable, crying: "What is this, ye laggard spirits?

what negligence, what tarrying is this? Haste to the mount and strip you of the slough, that lets not God be manifest to you."

As doves when gathering wheat or tares, all assembled at their repast, quiet and showing not their wonted pride,

if aught be seen whereof they have fear, straightway
let stay their food, because they are assailed by greater
care;

so saw I that new company leave the singing, and go
towards the hillside, like one who goes, but knoweth
not where he may come forth;

nor was our parting less quick.

Purg. II, 106–133

The scene begins with an embrace—the first unre-
strained gesture of mutual affection between the pilgrim
and any member of the otherworld. Incomplete as it is,
the embrace stands out, first, by reason of its simple dramatic effectiveness: the strength of the impulse that moves
Casella forward with arms outstretched even before he
speaks; and the strength of its effect: the pilgrim steps
forward to embrace Casella without recognizing him at
all, impelled by the force of the other's shown affection.
But it stands out, too, because like the natural light
streaming over the scene, it contradicts Hell. Hell was full
of barriers and angry approaches or retreats; the last time
the pilgrim reached out to touch one of the dead, it was
to tear out Bocca degli Abati's hair.[2] With Casella's embrace, personal though it is, the lesson of *caritas* begins,
teaching that outgoing love for the whole created universe
which is to culminate in the final moment of Paradise.

Brief as it is, the passage is very rich in suggestion. It
touches off, for example, a resonance from the fifth canto
of the *Inferno*—from Francesca's half-deluded words,
"Amor che a nullo amato amar perdona . . ." which seem
almost to be acted out here as the recipient of love moves
irresistibly forward to respond. But—the new setting acts
like a new harmony applied to a melodic phrase, giving a
totally fresh and perhaps quite different view of the com-
manding power of love. It is fraternal love and not *Amor*
that impels Casella towards the pilgrim; and it is music, a
spiritual stuff rather than a material (the "fair body" of
Francesca) that motivated their living friendship, and

[2] *Inf.* XXXII, 97 ff.

now resumes its hold. Casella and the pilgrim love each other here with no material charm of any sort to bind them, and without infringing on anything—except, very slightly, the urgency with which each has been desiring to set off uphill.

In darting forward to embrace the stranger merely because the stranger has reached out towards him, he acts well—for what he sees and what he responds to here are one thing: a soul. It is not wrong to wish to embrace a soul (except in so far as it may be wrong to attempt the impossible; and here the poor pilgrim has simply forgotten the facts); but had it been wrong, the nature of the place would have saved him quite as surely as the nature of the world imperils him: his hands pass through the shadowy substance of Casella three times, returning to him empty.

The pathos of this failure is a third reason why the gesture of love between the pilgrim and Casella stands out. Human arms cannot lay hold of the unfleshed soul. In Purgatory spirit must learn to salute spirit in its own terms. To be sure, this is what the spirit had wanted—that of Casella, who is a shade, as well as that of the living man, who is travelling here in order to learn the nature and the uses of this road. It had craved its "coming out of exile" into this new world of self-regeneration. But nothing is more characteristic of Dante than his ability to express simultaneously this sense of release into the freedom of pure spirit, and a contrary sense—a nostalgic "memory" of the sweetness of physical human touch.[3]

In the soul's spontaneous step towards the pilgrim and the living man's irresistible response there is a quick summary of all the tenderness and pathos of the loving human gesture, together with the first warning of its doom

[3] It is important as we read this early portion of the *Purgatorio*, not to deform Dante by reading into him ideas that may belong to his sources, but which we do not actually find in him. I would merely point out here that there is no contempt for the body in him, and no yearning for the life after death as superior to the life in flesh. In the one as in the other there are, as he shows us, torment, regeneration and bliss. What Dante does say is that the spirit is an unruly team-mate for the body, and requires an immense self-discipline to attain its own end of well-being.

in the adult soul. The reaching out to clasp another in one's arms still carries its meaning, but it has lost its power. Casella, when he "smiles and draws back" after the pilgrim's futile clasping, recognizes and accepts this, as the bewildered pilgrim cannot yet do. (And the reader, even while he delights in that very phrase: "the shade smiled and drew back", can no more accept it than the pilgrim.) But Casella knows, in compensation for what he has lost, that love stands clear. His words will echo in many places throughout Purgatory: "Even as I loved thee in the mortal body, so do I love thee freed;" and will be remembered in Paradise where such love increases.

From the embrace and recognition, the scene advances easily and pacifically through the mutual questioning on how each came to be here at the foot of the mountain at this moment, to the high point of the pilgrim's request that Casella sing for him. Once again, by this innocent audacity, the sweetness of human things is brought forward in the moment of pause before the grave business of the mountain begins. Everything in the passage conspires to bring this sweetness home: the pilgrim's words— "that song of love which was wont to calm my every desire"; the position of those words, following directly on Casella's description of the dead waiting at Tiber's mouth; and the song itself with its frail, perilous reality here, beyond death. The souls should not be stopping to listen to a song. They should be searching out their path; they know that. They have left the world of song-making behind; the pilgrim knows that when he says "If a new law take not from thee memory or skill in that song . . ." But what the poem says is that a lyric and a melody made by men can be so powerful in their beauty that the distress of the journey through Hell and the distress of the passage through death can be forgotten in hearing them. More than that: momentarily the road that leads to Heaven can be forgotten.

Casella sings. The lyric he chooses is by the young Dante: *Amor che nella mente mia ragiona . . .* and this in itself adds a further, tender and persuasive human touch to the scene. The souls newly arrived in Purgatory, who have just finished singing the hymn *In exitu Israel,* listen raptly. So do Virgil and his pupil. And thus they all hang back from the mountain until Cato shouts sense at them and, instantly, they disperse. It is an interesting afterthought that the poem Casella sings is one that makes much of the connection between earthly beauty and the divine.[4] Yet here, where the work of returning to the source of beauty and wisdom begins, it figures as one of those "toys" which men have made "for the delight of the eye, copying the outward forms of the things they make, but inwardly forsaking Him by whom they were made and destroying what they themselves have been made to be"![5]

The scene that ends with Cato's rebuke is a curious and characteristic mixture—literally, part fresh wonder and delight in the new journey towards God, part nostalgia for the world; but figuratively (in so far as Purgatory is a stage in life itself), a recognition of recovery from wrong love and a celebration of the permanent goods of fraternal love and of the creative insight. It is for the pilgrim a gentle pause between the terribleness of Hell and the austerities of the purgatorial climb, the tears of Hell and the disciplines of the mountain—a pause where human attachment to the substantial forms of cherished things—the friend, the song—asserts itself briefly and innocently. In the *Comedy,* with all its sternness towards the offences by which men destroy themselves, there is a store of such redeeming memories. None matches this for limpid clarity and tenderness.

SECOND MEETING: SORDELLO

Purgatorio's second meeting of poets (Canto VI, 61 ff.) is played in a totally different atmosphere and with a different preoccupation from the first, although once again

[4] The second Ode of Dante's *Convivio*
[5] St Augustine, *The Confessions,* Bk. X, chap. 34; Library of Christian Classics, vol. 7, Philadelphia, Westminster Press

the visible action centres in an embrace and affirms fraternal love. The travellers have climbed the first slopes of the mountain, but have not yet reached the gates of Purgatory proper. On these slopes all those who died excommunicate or were late in repentance are waiting out their penalty of delayed admission, in a kind of enforced meditative idleness. Virgil and the pilgrim have stopped to talk with many of them. When the sixth canto opens they are breaking away with some difficulty from a crowd of eager penitents who have besieged the living man to carry news of them back to earth so that prayers may be said for them. The two poets escape at last and walk on alone, gladly. The pilgrim poses a serious question on the nature of prayer, and Virgil answers. The reader listens. For a while no new appeal is made to the eye, which is aware of nothing except the two solitary figures walking on a shadowed road beside a steep cliff. Then a third figure comes into view. Virgil notes it: "But see there a soul which, placed alone, solitary, looketh towards us; it will point out to us the quickest way."

With the approach to this soul the verse changes altogether in character. It has been, since the lone walk began, inconspicuous, efficient, dry—addressed to the intellect. But now, with one of those sudden redirections of attention with which Dante over and over again surprises and refreshes the reader's mind, he catches the eye again and brings it to bear on a sharply focussed, intensely arresting close view. At the same moment he begins to interest the ear with a matching eloquence of sound. (It is his way of introducing a dramatic action: he alerts the eye and the ear very precisely.) With "venimmo a lei", one is immediately aware again of *seeing* and *hearing* the poem.

> *Venimmo a lei. O anima lombarda,*
> *come ti stavi altera e disdegnosa,*
> *e nel mover delli occhi onesta e tarda!*

> *Ella non ci dicea alcuna cosa,*
> *ma lasciavane gir, solo sguardando*
> *a guisa di leon quando si posa.*

Pur Virgilio si trasse a lei, pregando
che ne mostrasse la miglior salita;
e quella non rispuose al suo dimando,

ma di nostro paese e della vita
c'inchiese; e 'l dolce duca incominciava
"Mantova . . .", e l'ombra, tutta in sè romita,

surse ver lui del loco ove pria stava,
dicendo: "O Mantovano, io son Sordello
della tua terra!" E l'un l'altro abbracciava.

We came to it: O Lombard soul, how wast thou haughty and disdainful, and in the movement of thine eyes majestic and slow!

Naught it said to us, but allowed us to go on, watching only after the fashion of a lion when he couches.

Yet did Virgil draw on towards it, praying that it would show to us the best ascent; and that spirit answered not his demand,

but of our country and our life did ask us. And the sweet Leader began: "Mantua . . ." and the shade, all rapt in self,

leapt towards him from the place where first it was, saying: "O Mantuan, I am Sordello of thy city." And one embraced the other.

VI, 61-75

How much is crowded into this passage! Virgil and the pilgrim are shown amiable, humble and trusting, intent only on getting accurate directions towards their goal. Sordello, remote, brooding, suspicious, is not at all interested in them until he has found *whence* they come. The two disparate moods and concerns (for goal, for source) give way with tremendous emotion before the single word: "Mantua . . ."

Sordello does not know the stranger who answers his question with "Mantua . . .", yet this city name brings him up to his feet from the place where he had sat "all

rapt in self", to fling himself on the other Mantuan's neck,
silencing whatever else the other Mantuan might have
been about to reveal to him. The "couching lion" springs
like a delighted lover. His gesture conveys a notable depth
of attachment to a native town, and of quickness to embrace a fellow-citizen whoever or whatever else he may
be, and whenever he may have lived. Sordello's haughty
brooding disappears instantly, as once again love for the
living world wells up in the afterworld, stating dramatically the force of its hold on the soul. "Mantua" has
broken through Sordello's self-communing and Virgil's interest in the road, much as Casella's song did through the
holy awe of souls and pilgrims newly arrived at the base
of the mountain.

This happens. Before the reader has time to reflect on
it (and perhaps to raise his eyebrows at such patriotism),
reflection is brought before him by a new voice. While
Sordello and Virgil are in each other's arms,[6] the scene
enters the second of its three distinct parts. Or rather, the
light fades from the stage and falls on the author of the
poem, who now from his place of writing makes a fierce
and bitter commentary:

> Ahi serva Italia, di dolore ostello,
> nave sanza nocchiere in gran tempesta,
> non donna di provincie, ma bordello!
>
> Quell'anima gentil fu così presta,
> sol per lo dolce suon della sua terra,
> di fare al cittadin suo quivi festa;
>
> e ora in te non stanno sanza guerra
> li vivi tuoi, e l'un l'altro si rode
> di quei ch'un muro ed una fossa serra.
>
> Cerca, misera, intorno dalle prode
> le tue marine, e poi ti guarda in seno,
> s'alcuna parte in te di pace gode.

---

[6] The disaster of the pilgrim's attempt to embrace Casella is
not repeated because both Virgil and Sordello are shades.

Ah Italy, thou slave, hostel of woe, vessel without pilot in a mighty storm, no mistress of provinces, but a brothel!

That gentle spirit was thus quick merely at the sweet name of his city, to give greeting there to his fellow-citizen;

and now in thee thy living abide not without war, and one doth rend the other of those that one wall and one foss shuts in.

Search, wretched one, around thy seacoasts by the shores, and then gaze in thy bosom, if any part of thee enjoy peace.

VI, 76–87

The diatribe is long and impassioned. Dante does not very often interrupt the course of his narrative to comment on the action in his fully 'educated' voice—his voice from the world. The embrace of Sordello—a minute and touching demonstration of the unitive power of the political community, taking precedence over every individual concern—touches off Dante's hatred of its opposite: the nation as "brothel", where love is travestied and the ruling lady counts her coins. The voice grows vitriolic. It explores the relationship of Church and Empire, of ecclesiastic and civil government generally (a major theme of the *Comedy*), and recalls the argument of the *De Monarchia* for independent authority of the emperor in the civil realm. It scores the current emperor for his neglect of Italy, the political ambitiousness of the people, the feuds of the nobility. Its tone is by turns rough, pleading and—when finally the view narrows upon Florence, his own loved and loathed native city—bitingly ironic. Almost four times the length of the scene from which it springs as a commentary, this diatribe takes up the reader's whole attention and blots Sordello and Virgil out of thought. It brings the canto to an end.

With the opening of Canto VII the light again centres on the true stage, and the scene resumes exactly where it left off, regaining immediately its former large-paced dignity. Some twenty more verses bring the dramatic line of the meeting to an end.

> *Poscia che l'accoglienze oneste e liete*
> *furo iterate tre e quattro volte,*
> *Sordel si trasse e disse: "Voi, chi siete?"*

> *"Anzi che a questo monte fosser volte*
> *l'anime degne di salire a Dio,*
> *fur l'ossa mie per Ottavian sepolte.*

> *Io son Virgilio; e per null'altro rio*
> *lo ciel perdei che per non aver fè."*
> *Cosi rispuose allora il duca mio.*

> *Qual è colui che cosa innanzi a sè*
> *subita vede ond' e' si maraviglia,*
> *che crede e non, dicendo 'Ella è . . . non è . . .',*

> *tal parve quelli; e poi chinò le ciglia,*
> *e umilmente ritornò ver lui*
> *e abbracciòl là 've 'l minor s'appiglia.*

> *"O gloria de' Latin" disse "per cui*
> *mostrò ciò che potea la lingua nostra,*
> *o pregio etterno del loco ond' io fui,*

> *qual merito o qual grazia mi ti mostra?"*

After the greetings dignified and glad had been repeated three and four times, Sordello drew him back and said: "Who art thou?"

"Ere to this mount were turned those spirits worthy to ascend to God, my bones by Octavian had been buried.

I am Virgil; and for no other sin did I lose heaven than for not having faith": thus answered then my Leader.

As one who seeth suddenly a thing before him whereat he marvels, who believes, and believes not, saying: "It is, it is not";

such seemed he, and forthwith bent his brow and
humbly turned back towards my Leader, and embraced him where the inferior clasps.

"O glory of the Latins" said he, "by whom our tongue
showed forth all its power, O eternal praise of the
place whence I sprang,

what merit or what favor showeth thee to me?"
VII, 1–19

One sees only now with what cunning stagecraft Dante
placed his diatribe—interrupting the important sequence
of Sordello's two questions and two embraces; making the
reader forget the Mantuan before he had quite grasped
his meaning; and returning to him for this brief second
disclosure which throws so much light back upon the first.
Sordello's "Who art thou?" is asked some time after his
"where do you come from?" (indeed, rather long after, if
we measure by the poem rather than by clock), because it
involves a matter of secondary interest to him. After the
first question, the Mantuan embraces his co-citizen about
the neck, whoever he may be. When the second question
has been answered, it is the *poet* Sordello who clasps the
poet Virgil about the knees. But we must also note that
he clasps him with such humble reverence not because of
a personal bond (he does not love Virgil; he does not
share Dante's filial bond), but because Virgil is the "glory
of the Latins", the benefactor of "our tongue", and the
cause of signal honour to Mantua. These terms treat the
poet's achievement as a citizen's achievement. Personal
glory and the excellence of the work as Sordello himself
might have felt it, do not enter into question: Virgil's
task is seen exclusively as the Roman and imperial monu-
ment which assuredly it was. Thus one may say that the
entire scene, together with its interrupting diatribe, centres on the City or Nation, in three views corresponding
to its three sections: the city as it may be cherished by
its citizens; as it may be ill-governed civilly and ecclesiasti-
cally; and as it may be served by its artists.

The meeting with Sordello has affinities with Farinata's scene in Hell—resemblances that expand and confirm its meaning. Their political themes and their form (limitedly) relate them. Both protagonists appear first in isolation from others of their kind; both exhibit a haughty acceptance of their condition (Farinata "as if he entertained great scorn of Hell,"; Sordello "haughty and disdainful" as he waits outside the Purgatory gates); the first words in which each addresses the visitors show their primary concern with native place: Farinata, recognizing the pilgrim by his speech as a fellow-Tuscan, hails him and then questions: "Who were thy forebears?"; Sordello, approached by Virgil, asks both pilgrims "of our city and our life", and only later enquires "Who art thou?" Upon this base of likeness in the deep patriotic concern of each, rise two contrary developments: the one full of the pain of partisan antagonism, the other of delight in the tie of place-allegiance; the first a partisan clash, returning ferociously to particular and local issues until even the sinner wearies of his rage—the second centring on the repeated gesture of embrace, a recognition and honouring of co-citizen and forerunner in civic poetry, without reference to the specific political concerns which may have agitated either man during his lifetime.

Surely Dante had Farinata in mind when he composed the Sordello episode, and possibly he hoped that his reader would remember that he had in Hell been shown great patriotism deviated into destructive factionalism, and would be aware of the almost graphic contrasting of the dispute below with the embrace above. And this might lead the reader to a further observation: for all that Sordello's love is the corrective of Farinata's disdain towards a fellow-citizen, it, too, is touched with partisanship; it, too, is based on a specific and restricting bond—on Mantua, and the "glory of the Latins". It is a good beginning of love, but still too narrow. Inside Purgatory's gates such local and specific attachments will loosen their grip in a larger perspective; they will no longer take first place. Casella's music has already faded from the ears that stopped so eagerly to listen to it; and the sort of passion Sordello feels for his native city will have to be laid aside, too. There will be no room for either on the way up the mountain where souls learn to transcend the restrictions that are in such loves. Because of this, and because the world that generates them is still so close, a certain pathos touches every reminder of them here in the foothills. That pathos clings round the image of Sordello kneeling to clasp Virgil's knees because he has shed an endless renown on Mantua. But it will be dispersed. The "little bark" of Dante's wit, which as it goes continually casts its light back over its own wake, will later give a new light on Sordello's close Mantuan feelings. On the Terrace of the Envious, an anonymous soul will gently rebuke the pilgrim for asking whether anybody in that place is an Italian. He will say:

> O frate mio, ciascuna è cittadina
> d'una vera città; ma tu vuo' dire
> che vivesse in Italia peregrina."

"O my brother, each of us is a citizen of one true city; but you must mean to ask if any of us lived as a pilgrim in Italy."[7]

Thereafter in Purgatory such questions will not be asked.

THIRD MEETING: STATIUS

Again the overt action of the scene centres in a joyous recognition and an embrace which, in this third meeting, is sketched but not completed. As in the second meeting, the tribute of love and admiration is for Virgil, and comes from a poet of his own country who lived after him. The construction of the scene in an initial encounter, a central discourse of some length, and a postponed and intensely moving recognition, is reminiscent of that in the second meeting. These are the external links. The internal con-

[7] XIII, 94-96 (author's tr.)

nections are more important. They carry forward the exploration of fraternal love within the corrective gates of Purgatory, and affirm again in a new way the undiminishable value of life to the living and to the dead.

Virgil and the pilgrim have now completed more than half their journey inside the gates of Purgatory, and are about to leave the fifth Terrace. As they walk, skirting the prostrate forms of those who are in penitence for avarice and prodigality, the two travellers ponder on the quaking of the mountain and the many-voiced cry of *Gloria in excelsis Deo* which had stopped them in amazement just a moment since.[8] The pilgrim is burning, not with curiosity but with "the natural thirst which never is sated save with the water whereof the poor Samaritan woman asked the grace", when

> *Ed ecco, sì come ne scrive Luca*
> *che Cristo apparve a' due ch'erano in via,*
> *già surto fuor della sepulcral buca,*
>
> *ci apparve un'ombra, e dietro a noi venìa,*
> *dal piè guardando la turba che giace;*
> *nè ci addemmo di lei, sì parlò pria,*
>
> *dicendo: "O frati miei, Dio vi dea pace".*

Lo, even as Luke writes to us Christ appeared to the two who were on their way, already arisen from the mouth of the tomb,

a shade appeared to us, and came on behind us, gazing at its feet on the prostrate crowd, nor did we perceive it until it first spake,

saying, "My brothers, God give you peace."

XXI, 7–12

Virgil returns this hallowed greeting[9] and explains at once, with his usual impeccable consideration for the right understanding of others, that neither he nor his companion is making the mountain journey in Statius' sense.

[8] XX, 124
[9] The words are Jesus', according to Luke xxiv, 36.

Statius shows no astonishment. The three do not pause at
all to exchange these civilities, but rather continue "sturdily" on their road, questioning and answering one another
as they go. The pilgrim's burning "thirst" is slaked by the
newcomer: the trembling of the mountain, he says, was
not earthquake (nor could have been, since Purgatory
stands out of reach of the earth's physical events), but
was the concrete expression of a spiritual occurrence; the
whole mountain's concerted joy in the rising of a single
soul from one of the purgatorial disciplines. And that soul
rose, as is the way here, at the simple and unprompted
dictate of its own will, knowing itself cleansed. Statius
adds, as though it were a trifling matter, that he himself
was the soul whose rising from the fifth Terrace has so
astonished Virgil and the pilgrim.

40   *Quei cominciò: "Cosa non è che sanza*
            ordine senta la religïone
            della montagna, o che sia fuor d'usanza.

        Libero è qui da ogni alterazione:
            di quel che 'l ciel da sè in sè riceve
            esser ci puote, e non d'altro, cagione.

        Per che non pioggia, non grando, non neve,
            non rugiada, non brina più su cade
            che la scaletta di tre gradi breve:

        nuvole spesse non paion nè rade,
            nè coruscar, nè figlia di Taumante,
            che di là cangia sovente contrade:

                .   .   .   .   .

58   *Tremaci quando alcuna anima monda*
            sentesi, sì che surga o che si mova
            per salir su; e tal grido seconda.

        Della mondizia sol voler fa prova,
            che, tutto libero a mutar convento,
            l'alma sorprende, e di voler le giova.

        Prima vuol ben, ma non lascia il talento
            che divina giustizia, contra voglia,
            come fu al peccar, pone al tormento.

67   *E io, che son giaciuto a questa doglia*
        cinquecent'anni e più, pur mo sentii
        libera volontà di miglior soglia:

    Però sentisti il tremoto e li pii
        spiriti per lo monte render lode
        a quel Segnor che tosto su li 'nvii."

    Così ne disse; e però ch'el si gode
        tanto del ber quant'è grande la sete,
        non saprei dir quant'el mi fece prode.

    E 'l savio duca: "Omai veggio la rete
        che qui v'impiglia e come si scalappia,
        perchè ci trema, e perchè congaudete.

    Ora chi fosti, piacciati ch'io sappia,
        e perchè tanti secoli giaciuto
81   *qui se', nelle parole tue mi cappia."*

That spirit began: "The holy rule of the mount suffereth naught that is arbitrary, or that is outside custom.

Here it is free from all terrestrial change; that which Heaven receives into itself from itself may here operate as cause, and naught else:

since neither rain, nor hail, nor snow, nor dew, nor hoar-frost, falls any higher than the short little stairway of the three steps.

Clouds dense or thin appear not, nor lightning flash, nor Thaumas' daughter, who yonder oft changes her region.

. . . . .

It quakes here when some soul feeleth herself cleansed, so that she may rise up, or set forth, to mount on high, and such a shout follows her.

Of the cleansing the will alone gives proof, which fills the soul, all free to change her cloister, and avails her to will.

She wills indeed before, but that desire permits it
not which divine justice sets, counter to will, towards
the penalty, even as it was towards the sin.

And I who have lain under this torment five hundred years and more, only now felt free will for a better threshold.

Therefore didst thou feel the earthquake, and hear
the pious spirits about the mount give praises to that
Lord—soon may he send them above."

Thus he spake to us; and since we enjoy most the
draught in proportion as our thirst is great, I could
not tell how much he profited me.

And the wise Leader: "Now I see the net that catches
you here, and how one breaks through, wherefore it
quakes here, and whereat ye make glad together.

Now may it please thee that I know who thou wast:
and why thou hast lain here so many ages, let me learn
from thy words."

XXI, 40 ff.

The reader will have noted that he is here breathing a
different air from that of the earlier meetings—soberer,
more restrained, more intellectual: the air of Purgatory
proper. Nothing is left of that sense of dawning understanding and childlike innocence which dominated the
whole of Casella's tender encounter; and nothing of the
brooding aloofness which shielded the single-minded Sordello from the intrusions of strangers. What one saw in
the power of Casella's music at the foot of the hill, in
Belacqua's sloth,[10] in Sordello's lonely watchfulness, was
a weight of the world still holding the soul back—external
and accidental things still exercising their power to con-
fuse, to distract, to offend. Within the gates of Purgatory
such entrancements and broodings have no place; here all
is an orderly and measured activity and contemplation

[10] IV, 97 ff.

which mend what has been marred, and get the soul in
readiness for its more perfect and final action of understanding and love. Statius walks his way "sturdily", without asking who the visitors may be; and one feels that the
mountain has matured him, and that his present compo-
sure will never again be ruffled. Indeed, the whole stretch
of the canto between lines 1 and 100 is notably impersonal, grave, religious. Nothing happens. Nothing thrills
the imagination unless retrospectively (the thrilling quake
and the cry of *Gloria* are merely *recalled* here), and the
reader is sobered—possibly even a little dulled. Such may
well be his feeling when he reaches the passage in which
Statius at last gives his identity:

> *"Nel tempo che 'l buon Tito, con l'aiuto*
> *del sommo rege, vendicò le fora*
> *ond'uscì 'l sangue per Giuda venduto,*
>
> *col nome che più dura e più onora*
> *era io di là" rispuose quello spirto*
> *"famoso assai, ma non con fede ancora.*
>
> *Tanto fu dolce mio vocale spirto,*
> *che, tolosano, a sè mi trasse Roma,*
> *dove mertai le tempie ornar di mirto.*
>
> *Stazio la gente ancor di là mi noma:*
> *cantai di Tebe, e poi del grande Achille;*
> *ma caddi in via con la seconda soma.*
>
> *Al mio ardor fuor seme le faville,*
> *che mi scaldar, della divina fiamma*
> *onde sono allumati più di mille;*
>
> *dell'Eneïda dico. . . ."*

"What time the good Titus with the help of the Highest King avenged the wounds whence issued the blood
by Judas sold,

with the name which most endures and honours
most," answered that spirit, "I was yonder, great in
fame, but not yet with faith.

So sweet was the music of my words that me, a
Toulousian, Rome drew to herself, where I did merit
a crown of myrtle for my brow.

Statius folk yonder still do name me; I sang of Thebes,
and then of the great Achilles; but I fell by the way
with the second burden.

The sparks which warmed me, from the divine flame,
whence more than a thousand have been kindled,
were the seeds of my poetic fire;

Of the Aeneid I speak. . . ."

XXI, 82–97

It is not a lively passage. The two circumlocutions at
the beginning make it cumbersome; its metaphors seem
worn; until it reaches the subject of the *Aeneid* it is merely
a heavily ornamented, short, factual autobiography. One
is certainly not attracted to the speaker. At most one allows
him dignity and impersonal honesty. But we are bound to
look at him a little more closely.

The poet Statius was born in Naples early in the first
century A.D., and died probably before the year 100.[11] If
we suppose that souls were not admissible to Purgatory
before the first professing Christians died, he must then
have come to the mountain among the first few genera-
tions of penitents, and must have climbed very slowly indeed—perhaps rooting out other evil dispositions as length-
ily as that of prodigality, which, as he will tell Virgil, it
took him five hundred years to cure. There is, of course, no
standard average speed for this journey. But evidently we
are intended to feel that Statius' labour has been long—
that centuries have passed over him and troops of souls
passed by him as he worked out his penance. All during
the climb the pilgrim has talked to no one of comparable
age, while on the other hand some persons whose deaths
he remembers well (Forese Donati, Guido Guinizelli)

---

[11] Dante was mistaken in thinking him born in Toulouse. The
two works which Statius here mentions, his *Thebaid* and his *Achil-
leid*, were both much read in the Middle Ages. They are a frequent
source of myths in the *Comedy*.

have already reached the highest terraces. Taking note of Statius' great age and heavy penance, we might well expect in him a certain remoteness from men and from the world's affairs. To all this his ponderousness of speech is appropriate.

What is more, since Statius has now completed his penances (he has no stay to make on the last two terraces), he must have learned all that the mountain has to teach him, except the lesson of the flames through which every soul must pass in leaving Purgatory. Sober with this learning, he can himself no longer feel anything "that is without order". And as the caprices of inanimate nature are unable to touch the mountain, so, evidently, the quirks of "natural" desire cannot any longer affect the soul which has absorbed the mountain's teaching. Nothing is in him "save that which Heaven receives into itself from itself"[12]— namely, eternal substance and the idea of the good. In Statius, then, all conflict between desire and will is ended; he is beyond all moral lapse, beyond suffering (save from the seventh Terrace flames), beyond the fascination of "present things with their false pleasure",[13] and therefore safe from illusion.

Obviously Dante has here chosen difficult material: a protagonist in whom there is no longer any cause for struggle, no possibility of temptation, no charm of perilous ignorance: an austere, simple, measured, passionless figure.

Everything in those opening passages which we have already reviewed, works to achieve this austere tonality and to suggest an almost complete transcendence of personal and worldly concerns: the rapid pace of the soul, concentrated on his goal; the consecrated greeting, and the comparison to one who has risen beyond death;[14] the benign incuriosity towards the strangers; the measured discourse on the ordering of desire and will; the total objectivity of his references to himself. In effect, it is as though time and penitence had dimmed out in Statius all vibrancy towards the past, and memory, which spoke out so sweetly and poignantly about the living world in Casella and Sordello

[12] Purg. XXI, 44   [13] Purg. XXXI, 34   [14] Purg. XXI, 7–9

(and so bitterly and poignantly in others—Marco Lombardo[15] and Hugh Capet,[16] for example), had in this penitent reduced her voice to a tranquil whisper.

I think that this, or something very like it, is what Dante intends us to feel in the first part of Statius' self-identifying speech—which comes late, and only then in answer to an explicit question from Virgil. He wants us to feel, first, this closed, ascetic, ancient man in whom the world, as he knew it, has become a mere formal memory. But having established that figure in our minds, Dante means to surprise us a little—by showing that at one point Statius' memory and emotion still have keenness. At that point a poem, the *Aeneid*, wakes in him an expression that is personal and vivid:

> *"Dell'Eneida dico, la qual mamma*
> *fummi e fummi nutrice poetando:*
> *sanz'essa non fermai peso di dramma."*

"Of the Aeneid I speak, which was a mother and was to me a nurse in poesy; without it I had not stayed the weight of a drachm."

97–99

Mother and nurse! They are strong words. Mother and nurse are maker and preserver. And equally strong is the continuing image of the succoured infant in "without it I had not stayed the weight of a drachm". The *Aeneid* is mother and nurse of Statius' real life, the one he *can* remember, which is that of poetry. Love for poetry is love for truth and wisdom, thus in harmony with the soul's right goal—in harmony with heaven. The last words of Statius' speech take us even further. For the *Aeneid*, experienced as a great work of art, has generated in Statius a love for its maker so powerful that it has survived, as nothing else has, all the long disciplines of time and penitence. And this love is so strong that "to have known Virgil" is a desire which not even the twelve centuries have been able to erase. Nor does this contradict the spirit of

15 *Purg.* XVI, 25 ff.   16 *Purg.* XX, 40 ff.

the journey; for this love is a small but instructive analogue of the greater one by which the human creature reading the "book" of the universe[17] comes to love and to search for the supreme author, whose "art"[18] adorns earth and the heavens. Thus the startling assertion of Statius' final lines is not so much a lapse into, as a bold profession of lofty personal devotion: "And to have lived yonder when Virgil was alive, I would consent to one more sun than I owe to my coming forth from exile."

The whole meaning as well as the dramatic impulse of the scene begins with these lines. What is portrayed here is the crucial movement in Statius from a neutral reverence to a burst of fraternal love, coloured by what is both innocent and intensely personal in the bonds that make one man peculiarly dear to another wherever they may be —even in the high spheres of heaven.[19] It is as though the composed face of the ascetic were here broken to show us a momentary glimpse of the characterizing feature of his being.

Note, too, the price Statius would pay for meeting face to face with Virgil. He is almost at the end of his purgatorial journey. On the way he has suffered, and he still suffers, continual thirst for what lies ahead. In Paradise he will reach eternal slaking of all thirsts. Yet this soul, for whom life is now only a memory, would if he could alter *that memory*[20] to include Virgil in it, willingly pay an added year of painful delay to flawless bliss. His wish, then, is a marvellous absurdity. Absurd, in that it offers an enor-

---

[17] See *Par.* XII, 121 for one of the lesser "books", and *Par.* XXXIII, 85–87. The analogy was a familiar one in Dante's time. Cf. Hugh of St Victor: "For the whole visible world is as a book written by the finger of God, that is, created by divine power."

[18] See *Par.* IX, 106 and X, 10

[19] Cf. in the *Paradiso*, Cacciaguida's delight in the pilgrim: Cantos XV, XVI. Cf. also *Par.* XXXI, 31 ff.

[20] Note the tense of the verb *assentirei* (I would consent) in line 101. He does not say: to have lived yonder when Virgil was alive I *would have* consented . . . etc. Thus, unless the tense is inadvertent, it is indeed the mere memory Statius would pay so dearly for.

mous sacrifice for a reward which will soon cease to be coveted. But marvellous in the extraordinary value set upon the prize of *being able to remember Virgil*. And marvellous in the poetry that expands from the simple statement of such longing for such a prize. *To have a more perfect memory of life is worth a delay of divine experience*. And how could this be, were not life itself the very key to unlock the divine? In this ending of Statius' speech, love of the living contact with living things wells up again, contrary to every expectation, and colours the rational framework of the ascent.

No pause is given, no astonishment expressed at this remarkable confession. Virgil, whose tact in every situation is immense, will not break through the penitent's disciplined ardour for an idea, with a crass "I am he!" It is a final grace of the scene that when the revelation does come it is forced by an expressive gesture, a flash of the still spontaneous emotionality of the imperfect, living pilgrim.

> *Volser Virgilio a me queste parole*
> *con viso che, tacendo, disse 'Taci';*
> *ma non può tutto la virtù che vole;*
>
> *chè riso e pianto son tanto seguaci*
> *alla passion di che ciascun si spicca,*
> *che men seguon voler ne' più veraci.*
>
> *Io pur sorrisi come l'uom ch'ammicca;*
> *per che l'ombra si tacque, e riguardommi*
> *nelli occhi ove 'l sembiante più si ficca;*
>
> *e "Se tanto labore in bene assommi"*
> *disse, "perchè la tua faccia testeso*
> *un lampeggiar di riso dimostrommi?"*
>
> *Or son io d'una parte e d'altra preso:*
> *l'una mi fa tacer, l'altra scongiura*
> *ch'io dica; ond'io sospiro e sono inteso*
>
> *dal mio maestro, e "Non aver paura"*
> *mi dice "di parlar; ma parla e digli*
> *quel ch' e' dimanda con cotanta cura."*

Ond'io: "Forse che tu ti maravigli,
antico spirto, del rider ch'io fei;
ma più d'ammirazion vo' che ti pigli.

Questi che guida in alto li occhi miei,
è quel Virgilio dal qual tu togliesti
forza a cantar delli uomini e de' dei.

Se cagion altra al mio rider credesti,
lasciala per non vera, ed esser credi
quelle parole che di lui dicesti."

Già s'inchinava ad abbracciar li piedi
al mio dottor, ma el li disse: "Frate,
non far, che tu se' ombra e ombra vedi."

These words turned Virgil to me with a look that silently said: "Be silent." But the virtue which wills is not all powerful;

for laughter and tears follow so closely the passion from which each springs, that they least obey the will in the most truthful.

I did but smile, like one who makes a sign; whereat the shade was silent and looked at me in the eyes, where most the soul is fixed.

And he said: "So may such great toil achieve its end; wherefore did thy face but now display to me a flash of laughter?"

Now am I caught on either side; one makes me keep silence, the other conjures me to speak; wherefore I sigh and am understood

by my Master, and he said to me, "Have no fear of speaking, but speak, and tell him that which he asketh with so great desire."

Wherefore I: "Perchance thou dost marvel, O ancient spirit, at the laugh I gave, but I desire that yet greater wonder seize thee.

He who guideth mine eyes on high is that Virgil from
whom thou drewest power to sing of men and gods.

If thou didst believe other cause for my laughter, set
it aside as untrue, and believe it was those words
which thou spakest of him."

Already was he stooping to embrace my Teacher's
feet; but he said: "Brother, do not so, for thou art a
shade and a shade thou seest."

XXI, 103–132

There is a quick vivacity, a welling up of living freshness
in that brief pantomime between the pilgrim and Statius.
Caught off guard by the pilgrim's unexpected smile, the
heaven-bound penitent asks a very personal, limited, human question: why did you laugh just now? And in that
instant the reader feels poignantly both the tremendous
dignity of the ancient shade and the little lightning-stroke
power of a smile. Statius is no longer flat or pompous. It
is still an unquenched human impulse to which he responds when he bends to embrace Virgil's feet and that
resident of Limbo calls him back, reminding him of what
both now are. The scene resolves in Statius' acceptance:

> *Ed ei surgendo: "Or puoi la quantitate*
> *comprender dell'amor ch'a te mi scalda,*
> *quand'io dismento nostra vanitate*
> *trattando l'ombre come cosa salda."*

And he, rising: "Now canst thou comprehend the
measure of the love which warms me towards thee,
when I forget our nothingness,
and treat shades as a solid thing."

133–136

Words that end a scene, but remain in mind, expanding
in meaning, and peculiarly quickened by a double sense of
which, as we read, we are absently aware.

In the poem, figuratively, Dante intends Purgatory as a
stage in life, as also he intended Hell. If its people are
shades, that is because, by comparison with their strong
confidence in the power and reality of concrete things, men

are indeed frail, impalpable and ineffectual. They seem
to grow a little wiser about this with experience of life.
(Casella has learned some of the truth and Statius a great
deal.) But they forget it with every least jarring of attention, until the Purgatorial journey is completed. They want
not only to "see Virgil" alive, but to touch him, to kneel
at his feet, as though love got its reality from its embodiment. In the *literal* story before us Statius still feels this
way, and supposes that things would be quite altered and
his embrace of Virgil quite another matter, were he and
Virgil alive on earth and wearing solid bodies. In the *figurative* story, however, Statius' last words say a very different
thing: that *all* bodies are shades, and that their gestures
will neither add to nor subtract, by the weight of a
drachm, from the truth of love. Like an iridescent silk
these last lines of Canto XXI shimmer with both meanings simultaneously.[21]

[21] The meeting as "scene" may be said to end here, at the end
of Canto XXI. But there is a footnote to it in the following canto
which may concern the reader of these essays. It is Virgil's declaration of his affection for Statius (XXII, 10–17) beginning:
"Love kindled by virtue, hath ever kindled other love, if but its
flame were shown forth". I have already alluded to these lines
in the discussion of Francesca da Rimini's "Love, which to no
loved one permits excuse from loving", for the two lines are mu-
tually illuminating. In the dark light of Hell Francesca took all
love to be irresistible—an idea which would not have withstood
inspection, but which even the reader swallows at that point, along
with the canto's philtre. In the bright light of upper Purgatory
Virgil can say what he has known all along: that love is irresistible
when it is directed towards the good, kindled by *virtù*. Both Pilgrim and reader should now be prepared to understand him, for
he has already taught, in an open lesson on love, the nature of
our control over it (XVIII, 49–73).
   Statius' love for Virgil is kindled by *virtù*. Sordello's, perhaps,
too. But the difference between them tells us much about the
Purgatorial education in love. The three things for which Sordello
loved the older poet are, each to a given degree, local and restricted: his Mantuan origin, his glorification of Mantua, and his
ennobling of the Latin tongue. Statius, to be sure, *could* not have
loved Virgil for the Mantuan reasons; yet what signifies is rather
that he *did* love him for larger ones: for having kindled the
poetic fire in Statius himself and in "more than a thousand"

FOURTH MEETING: GUIDO GUINIZELLI

(*Canto XXV*, 109–XXVI, 148)

"And now we had come to the last turning . . ." and
"*Summae Deus clementiae* I then heard sung in the heart
of the great burning . . .". On the terrace of the Lustful,
in the midst of the fire that burns away the last traces of
human covetousness, there are no tears and no struggle;
emotion is stilled, and drama, for these souls, is at an end.
This is the final discipline. Except for this—in so far as
the souls we see are engaged in it—the lessons of the mount
have all been learned. The whole tenor of the episode
that begins here is generated by the theme of soul-poise,
coming now to its final perfection. Even the still imperfect
living pilgrim, who has come a long way in understanding,
shows new self-mastery. Purgatory has been *his* struggle,
too: reason and action fighting the mountainous heaviness
of the will with its recoil into self-concern. Although for
him much struggle still lies ahead, he has won his way
up here: his will if not yet "free, upright and whole", as
Virgil will presently describe it,[22] is only one step short of
that. He is no longer timid (he has been walking alone
for some time, now) and no longer needs Virgil to cue him
into speech and nudge him to observation.

The dignity of the souls shows how far *they* have come;
they move quietly within the flames, and the voice of one
of them calls out for them all, hailing the pilgrim somewhat as Farinata did from the burning tomb in the sixth

---

others—thus as a poet, rather than as a national poet. Not only
will Mantua and the Latin tongue decline from living excellence
while the *Aeneid* continues to flourish among readers, but, as the
words of Beatrice and St Bernard in the *Paradiso* attest, poetry
as universalizing insight is blood kin to the insight of perfect wisdom, and will survive the world. And Statius loves Virgil for other
good reasons, as Canto XXII will show: for correcting his prodigality and for leading him towards Christianity. He loves him, in
short, not for the mortal ends he achieved, but for the paths he
opened towards the truth.   [22] *Purg.* XXVII, 140

Circle of Hell. Only, these souls are supported by a different strength: Farinata ignored his burning (and his companions) "as if he entertained great scorn of Hell", while Guinizelli and his companions seek the fire voluntarily, praising *summae Deus clementiae*. One desire holds them to their torture and makes them call out to the pilgrim, whose body they have recognized as a living one: their thirst to know and enter into the will of God. The pilgrim is a piece of evidence; the fire a preparation, scouring away the last stains of contrary desire.

The fire comes first, dominating the scene—a wall of flame fully surrounding the inner bank of the terrace in such a way that every soul, whether he stops to purge the taint of lust or not, must cross it to reach the stairway leading upward and outward. The pilgrim, too, if he is to reach the top of the mount, must pass it. We are not asked to see much else. The souls are visible only as dimly moving shapes within the flames; the pilgrim is skirting the dangerous outer edge of the cliff; Virgil has walked on a little ahead, absorbed in conversation with Statius.

Fire is the conventional symbol for love, hallowed by endless age and used as willingly by the Fathers of the Church as by the thirteenth-century lyric poets. Dante has never seriously thought of abandoning that convention, even in Hell. If we have been thrown off guard by the fires of the City of Dis, it is only because Dante has not yet there given us his broad definition of love as all desire directed towards that which we lack. According to this view, what moves the sinner towards his object is nothing other than love; and his pain in Hell is the burning of his unfulfilment. All love pains until it is resolved. Now, wherever there is a conflagration in the *Comedy* there is love-anguish. It is wrong love that scorches in Hell; at the passageway to Heaven it is right love, love for the One, for God. Right love, too, is painful at the moment when it takes hold, because it consumes to nothing every shred of self-concern, and redirects outward all the inward-turned tentacles of the soul. Right love, symbolized in the flame that ends the purgatorial climb, is selected by Dante as the special discipline for the Lustful because it offers the correct antidote to their poison, burning a small fire out with a great one, and setting men to cherish one another in spirit rather than to covet bodily.

Understanding this, the souls who have reached the seventh Terrace with this last and lightest burden of wrong love in them, cast themselves eagerly into "the heart of the great burning". What they master there is the culminating art of the reasonable mountain. There will be no more passion. All future ardour will be directed towards what cannot fail to reward it—whether the object bear the form of a lady or of an idea.

The material of the poem has become difficult. One might think it likely to founder in ideality or piety. But there is not the slightest danger of that. Dante's sure eye continues seeking and finding in human behaviour the real and recognizable gesture or attitude capable of revealing his psychology of love. Love of God does not, as we may have feared, result in a turning away from the world, but on the contrary a new and indestructible turning towards it in an emotion that bears comparison to nothing so much as to the feelings generated by the perfect work of art.

"Tell us how it is that thou makest of thee a wall against the sun, as if thou wert not yet caught within death's net."[23] A group of souls undoing the taint of carnal lust are walking along inside the fire, looking out. Still capable of feeling such wonder and delight in the presence of a living man that the burning does not hinder them, they stop to ask this question; and the single voice that speaks out for them all suggests both the general concern of the group for the highly graced stranger and, in the image of the net, their deep nostalgia for the bodies from which they have been cut off.

Still, they do not wait for their answer. A second troop of souls comes towards them, moving the opposite way through the flames, and they turn away instantly to embrace the newcomers.

[23] Purg. XXVI, 22-24

Lì veggio d'ogne parte farsi presta
ciascun'ombra e baciarsi una con una
sanza restar, contente a brieve festa:

così per entro loro schiera bruna
s'ammusa l'una con l'altra formica,
forse ad espiar lor via e lor fortuna.

There I see on either side each shade make haste to
kiss the other without staying, satisfied with short
greeting;

even so within their dark battalions one ant rubs
muzzle with another, perchance to spy out their way
and their fortune.

31–36

This kiss is a second example of the souls' power to
greet their joys in spite of anguish—and, indeed, in mitiga-
tion of anguish. Simultaneously it turns the reader's emotion away from the awfulness of the torment and towards
the sweetness of such fraternity. First he feels the sudden
shift from gravity to quaint freshness: the two troops of
the dead likened to the decent and industrious race of
ants; the souls reduced to miniatures by the comparison;
the quick and energetic kiss like a rubbing of ant-noses.
Then he is aware of the sense of the comparison (the ants
"kiss" with a view to feeling out their way) working on
the sense of the actual greeting, in which kissing has survived that carnality to which we attach it most, and now
marks the corrected form of love—fraternal *caritas*.
Fulfilling the ritual of the Terrace, the two throngs of
souls shout the examples of the sins they are purging:

la nova gente: "Soddoma e Gomorra";
e l'altra: "Nella vacca entra Pasife,
perchè 'l torello a sua lussuria corra."

Poi come grue ch'alle montagne Rife
volasser parte e parte inver l'arene,
queste del gel, quelle del sole schife,

l'una gente sen va, l'altra sen vene;
e tornan, lacrimando, a' primi canti
e al gridar che più lor si convene;

e raccostansi a me, come davanti,
essi medesmi che m'avean pregato,
attenti ad ascoltar ne' lor sembianti.

the new people, "Sodom and Gomorrah," and the
other: "Pasiphae enters the cow that the young bull
may haste her to lust."

Then, like cranes that should fly, some to the Rhi-
phean mountains, others towards the sands; these shy
of the frost, those of the sun,

the one people passes on, the other comes away, and
weeping they return to their former chants, and to
the cry which most befits them;

and those very same who had entreated me, drew
close to me as before, intent on listening in their
appearance.

40–51

Only twenty lines of verse have interrupted the pilgrim's
talk with the souls who first halted in the fire to question
him, but the effect is that of a long, crowded interlude,
so full is the passage of varied experiences. When all its
events and suggestions and patterns for the eye are completed (and one realizes that it was not an "interlude",
but the real business of the mountain that the souls trans-
acted here), the intensity of interest that still holds back
the small delaying group, still "intent on listening", seems
all the more poignant. Immersed in fire, they draw close
to the edge. The pilgrim answers their question: he is
indeed walking through their world alive, by an act of
grace; "Hence upward I go to be blind no longer". In his
turn he asks who they are, and what the troop is that
greeted and passed them in the fire.

They are for a moment as astonished and speechless as
the "dazed highlander" when he enters the city and looks

about him. When their bewilderment has passed, their spokesman answers. The pilgrim knows his voice well by now, but not his name, nor that this will matter to him far more than all the rest of what he may learn. He gets the answer to his question about the two troops of souls and learns the meaning of their ritual cries; and then:

> "Farotti ben di me volere scemo:
>   son Guido Guinizelli; e già mi purgo,
>   per ben dolermi prima ch'allo stremo."

"Thy desire of me I will indeed make to wane; Guido Guinizelli am I, and already purge me, because I full repentance made before the end."

91–93

This is by all means news to make the pilgrim startle. Guinizelli, who died in Dante's youth, before the flourishing of the "sweet new style" which he fathered, is the poet of his own era to whom the young Dante owed most. Even the twentieth-century reader is alerted when he names himself, expecting the pilgrim's emotion to make a touching scene.

But the Dante-pilgrim's response to the discovery that he is talking to the poet he cherishes so much is nothing at all like Sordello's outspoken joy or Statius' quick gesture of reverence on discovering Virgil. It is not a rush of delight, but a tangle of dark references and indirect discourse:

> Quali nella tristizia di Licurgo
>   si fer due figli a riveder la madre,
>   tal mi fec' io, ma non a tanto insurgo,
>
> quand'io odo nomar se stesso il padre
>   mio e delli altri miei miglior che mai
>   rime d'amore usar dolci e leggiadre;
>
> e sanza udire e dir pensoso andai
>   lunga fiata rimirando lui,
>   nè, per lo foco, in là più m'appressai.

Poi che di riguardar pasciuto fui,
   tutto m'offersi pronto al suo servigio
   con l'affermar che fa credere altrui.

As in the sorrow of Lycurgus two sons became on beholding again their mother, so became I, but not to
such height do I rise,

when I hear name himself the father of me and of
others, my betters, who ever used sweet and graceful
rhymes of love;

and without hearing and speaking, pondering I went,
long time gazing at him, nor because of the fire drew
I nigher thither.

When I was filled with beholding I offered me all
ready to his service, with the oath which compels another's belief.

                                        94–105

How many readers know—or even in the fourteenth century knew—the story of Lycurgus' sorrow? One turns hastily
to one's notes to learn it[24]—but the reference is still dark.
It remains somewhat dark to the reader of Statius'
Thebaid, where Dante got the legend. It takes some puzzling to discover that Dante is alluding here to the single
point in that story where Hypsipyle's two sons, discovering
their mother in the hands of the executioner (because, by
an act of carelessness she has brought about "Lycurgus'
sorrow"), rush forward to embrace her. Rather slowly it
emerges to one's understanding that the pilgrim feels a
similar impulse towards Guido, but does not "rise" to it
—on the face of things because the flames were more ter-
rifying to him than Hypsipyle's captors to her children.
According to his narrative, the pilgrim stops where he is
and stares silently for a while, absorbed in the sight of the

[24] Euridice, wife of Lycurgus the Nemean king, put their infant
son in the care of Hypsipyle, who abandoned him briefly in order
to assist the seven attackers of Thebes. The child perished of a
snake-bite during her absence. Hypsipyle was condemned to death.

master. Then he speaks—but Dante does not tell us what his words of devotion were, nor why he should have sworn an oath to bring home their truth. And yet he does give us Guinizelli's reply, which shows that they must have been strong and effective words: "thou leavest in me, by that which I hear, traces so deep and clear that Lethe cannot take them away nor make them dim." And Guinizelli adds: "if you spoke the truth, tell me what is the cause of so much affection for me?"

The pilgrim answers: "Your sweet ditties, which so long as modern use shall last, will make their very ink precious."

What has happened here to the emotional promise of the recognition? One feels that Dante has deliberately muffled the expectations raised by the "Guido Guinizelli am I . . ." in the mystification of the Lycurgus passage. He has given us a blurred indirect view of the pilgrim's access of feeling, pointedly withholding the sort of response which gave dramatic body to emotion in the preceding scenes. And if we read to the end of the canto we find that what follows continues to shift the narrative stress away from its emotional centre, and thus from its small dramatic potentiality. From Guido, recognized as the pilgrim's beloved master, the attention is turned by that poet himself, to a fellow-penitent—to Arnaut Daniel, the "better craftsman"; then to the question of common opinion and criticism. Guido vanishes. The pilgrim, left alone with Arnaut Daniel, speaks to him with gracious equanimity. Guido is forgotten in Arnaut's reply; and the canto ends as he, too, plunges deeper into the flames. There has been no drama and no explicit expression of emotion.

This is exactly what Dante intended. We are at the last parting between the soul and its reflex of dependence on the mortal body. This the poet has expressed by reducing the embrace between pilgrim and soul to a mere impulse in the living man, and by burying that impulse in the image of Lycurgus' prisoner and her sons; so that the reader, until he unravels the image, misses even the intention; but with the added effect that, when he has unravelled it, he feels in a peculiar way as though he were entering into the essence of the pilgrim's emotion. The whole structure of the passage—the pilgrim's silent amazement, his suppressed desire to rush forward and embrace Guido, the withholding of his actual words—tends to make the reader feel what he will subsequently understand: namely, the withering away of the need for the possessive grasping of love, and the beginning of the quiet poise of wisdom.

There has been no dramatic action in the fourth meeting because the souls are here cutting away the last traces of their capacity for human struggle, and the pilgrim has followed them in understanding. All four meetings have been pointing towards this conclusion. They have exhibited a progressive fading of emotional tension, as the desires that lead to human conflict were transformed and merged into the single fulfillable desire for perfect rational and intuitive vision. In this sense, the souls of the mountain go forward towards Paradise to be in the utterly satisfying presence of their true object eternally. And the pilgrim, who is still a man, moves forward towards his meeting with Beatrice, at last ready to know her without fear, shame, covetousness or capacity for loss.

At the point where we now stand, Hell, which was *all* conflicting desire (and all drama) is virtually blotted out. Casella's music, in which the repentant spirit rested and delayed, has, like Sordello's brooding aloofness, been left outside Purgatory's gates. Even Statius' slight lapse into forgetting *nostra vanitate* has become unlikely of repetition. So Dante shows us Guinizelli, halting to speak to the pilgrim, but without moving from the refining fire, and receiving the pilgrim's declaration of love only to point him on, through it, to a "better craftsman". And that craftsman, in whose words, veiled in the foreign provençal tongue, half the magic of the whole canto is vested, seems to speak for himself, for Guido, for every soul burning there. Tears and song are simultaneous. (*Ieu sui Arnaut, que plor e vau cantan.*) Weeping in the fire, he sees his "past madness", and, singing, his future joy. His warning is as much to the reader as the pilgrim: *Sovenha vos a temps de ma dolor*: see me burning here, and think twice of it.

The end of drama is not the end of love. Purgatorial discipline has not suppressed love, but on the contrary released it from passion and concentration. At once milder and stronger, open still to the special bonds of sympathy that bind one soul peculiarly to another within a universe of brotherhood, love is at last exempt from all personal craving and from vanity. The pilgrim's longing to rush through the flame to embrace Guinizelli marks the journey's last experience of the pathetic grounding of love in the sense of touch.

Chapter IV

BEATRICE

*When she walks on the glass pavement thou seest a
sun, a celestial sphere in the bosom of Idris.*

*When she kills with her glances, her speech restores to
life as though she, in giving life, were thereby Jesus.*

IBN ARABI

The would-be climber of Mt Purgatory is like the young
dancer: in order to become what he wills to be, he must
subject himself to endless hours of arduous labour, con-
tradicting at every turn the natural leanings of the heavy,
headstrong instrument he brings with him. But when the
soul comes forth at the top of the holy mountain, it wears
its seven virtues as naturally and unfalteringly as the perfected dancer does the elegance, suppleness and lightness
of his body.

At every terrace stop, and until they have passed
through the fire of the topmost, the souls continue to
suffer the heavy pull of desire against will. But when the
work is completed, will and desire flow together in harmony, and there is no longer in the whole capacity of the
spirit anything that might give rise to conflict. This is the
reason why drama, in so far as the souls are concerned,
has waned in Purgatory, burning itself out finally in the
achievement of *caritas* before the entryway to the garden
at the summit. What little further struggle the *Comedy*
contains must necessarily have its centre in the pilgrim,

whose final step in self-knowledge has not yet been taken.

Readers of the *Comedy* will recall that the last of the Purgatorial scenes discussed in the preceding chapter is not, in fact, the last dramatic encounter of the canticle. One might even say that the four meetings which that chapter stresses are overshadowed by the one which takes place beyond the flames, on the garden plateau. For this final meeting introduces the glorious Beatrice, towards whom the whole journey thus far has been aiming, under the impulse of the pilgrim's love and Heaven's grace.

So much has been written about this lady, she has been so laden with theories, printed notes, summaries and arguments, that it has become almost impossible for the present-day student of Dante to see her freshly as the text of the poem presents her. This situation is complicated by the undeniable fact that the totally uninstructed approach has great drawbacks, too. We cannot comprehend the Beatrice Dante had in mind without some notion of the mediaeval conceptions of woman and of love; we ought to know something of the poetry that preceded Dante's; and we need to have our eyes filled with mediaeval pictorial art, so that we will not visualize the scene in the Terrestrial Paradise in terms that give a false qualification (however beautiful) to the substance of Dante's vision.

Still, the reader who has little experience of these things can, if he hangs on closely to Dante's text, see the real outlines of the Beatrice image, and feel its poetry. He has chiefly to listen attentively to everything Dante says, and as carefully to avoid interpretations that contradict the spirit of the text or the important details of its letter. Dante is not careless or inconsequential: he says nothing unintentionally; and, since he wants us to know his meaning, he posts his poem with clues that can lead us to it. If that is so, whatever symbolic significance Beatrice is meant to have will be implicit in her whole figure and action, from the girlhood of the *Vita Nuova* onward, and will be capable of being *felt* as well as understood, without discords or contradictions. If we assume that this is so, we will not be tempted by artificial and academic interpreta-

tions or simple, sentimental ones, and will not seek a
"meaning" for Beatrice which is not promoted by the text
out of which she emerges. Above all, we will avoid the
deadly mistake of equating her with some noble and chill
abstract concept, as at times it has been the fashion to do.
For there is nothing to be gained but falsification and
diminishment of Dante's poetry by interpreting Beatrice
as an allegorical representation of Theology or Divine
Revelation, or any other abstraction of the sort. To do so
requires that one ignore a great many things that Dante
is at pains to impress on us (for surely it was not Theology
with which Dante fell in love at the age of nine, nor Revelation which descended into Hell to send Virgil to the
rescue, saying "It was love that moved me and that makes
me speak")—and above all, the exalted praise for the ca-
pacities of the human soul which is implied in her whole
role. As Etienne Gilson says,

> If Beatrice is only a symbol, she is a symbol whose
> body, after its death, was brought to earth, where it
> resides at the time when Dante was writing these
> lines (*Purg.* XXXI, 49–51) in expectation of its fu-
> ture glorification. We are assuredly yielding to the
> most urgent suggestions of Dante himself if we see in
> Beatrice a human being composed like us of a soul
> and a body, her soul being in heaven and her body
> on earth; a being who, since she is actually dead, has
> actually lived.[1]

This does not mean that the figure of Beatrice has no
symbolic import, but merely that it cannot have one
which contradicts the living past described in the *Vita
Nuova* and recalled vividly in the Terrestrial Paradise. The
risen and glorified Beatrice whom the protagonist had
loved during the brief lifetime described in the early
book, and who is the agent of his rescue in the *Comedy*,
is a figure that brims with significance. Her role is that of

[1] E. Gilson, *Dante the Philosopher* (Sheed and Ward, New
York 1949), p. 55. The reading of M. Gilson's whole superbly
ironic chapter is recommended.

a mediator between human and divine things. She is, as Virgil calls her, "a light between truth and intellect". But nothing in Dante's text or in his philosophy of composition will justify us in so forgetting the details of her well-established identity as to equate her with an abstraction, whatever its magnificence.

The reader will not even be tempted to make such an equation if he keeps the poem in view; Beatrice's voice and eyes and smile, as well as the rapture she arouses, are too much there to allow of forgetting them. The stock figure of allegory telescopes itself into the allegorical "meaning" and disappears soon from our thought; the image of Beatrice, on the contrary, is constantly enriched by the reflux of its wide range of meanings. Meanings which form the radiance of the literal figure, which are to be understood without a handbook of references, and which will be grasped in the same fundamental way by the reader, whether he knows little or much of mediaeval philosophy and theology. To say this is not by any means to prefer ignorance of these matters, but merely to advise sobriety in using them. For what really matters in reading the poem is to see the whole Beatrice as nearly as one may, and not an idea or a series of ideas derived from her and contemplated in detachment. Thus what must be considered first, and never lost sight of, is her whole role in the pilgrim's history and progress, to which she has been closely and personally related from his ninth year onward.

It is of course true that Dante asked us to read his poem on the four traditional levels of mediaeval allegory: literal, allegorical, moral and anagogical; and that Beatrice must have been meant to play her part on each. But these four levels form a structure based substantively on the first of them; and Dante's own instructions to us bear out the primary and inclusive nature of the literal. Speaking on the interpretation of poetry, generally, he says:

the literal sense should always come first, as the one in the meaning whereof the others are included, and

without which it were *impossible and irrational* to
attend to the others, especially to the allegorical.[2]

Of the *Comedy* specifically he remarks that it is upon and
about the literal sense of its subject that "the whole
progress of the work hinges".[3] Clearly it is Dante's intention that we hold to the literal Beatrice as matrix of whatever significance we may attach to her. We must obey him
in this. If not, we risk more than a mistaken symbolic interpretation: we risk missing much of the beauty of the
lyric poetry that surrounds Beatrice, and virtually all the
force of the dramatic characterization.

As I have noted, this literal Beatrice is no stranger to us
when, in the second canto of the *Inferno*, Virgil describes
her intercession for the pilgrim. The *Vita Nuova* had introduced her to Dante's readers as a young girl living in
her native city of Florence, had described the course of
the narrator's extraordinary love for her, announced her
untimely death and forecast her eternal glory. It had also
said about her some new and astonishing things which
carried forward by a leap of imaginative power and boldness the Platonizing lyric thought of the poetic school in
which Dante had formed his art. Beatrice's perfection in
every human quality was such that nothing more than her
presence and her greeting were needed to satisfy her lover.
Her beauty shed light on the beauty of other mortal objects. It pointed beyond itself, showing the way up the
Platonic ladder of being, to the ideas of truth, goodness,
beauty. It snatched the lover out of preoccupation with
himself and put his mind to making poetry in praise of
his lady. It centred him on what was enduring under the
cover of what perishes. It saved him from the world's illusion—or would have done so, then, in his early youth, if he
had not himself swerved from following, once Beatrice had
disappeared. It was, in a word (fulfilling the eternal function of love), the first great *eye-opener*.

This is perhaps as good a time as any to pause and
deliberate with those fairly numerous modern readers who

[2] *Convivio*, II, 1
[3] *Epistola* X (to Can Grande della Scala), section 8

declare themselves repelled by the hero's sexless love for the living girl in this story. Such repulsion generally represents a generalized personal conviction about the value of sexual desire and fulfilment in life. It is apt to go hand in hand with a failure to enter into the writer's reasons for omitting these things or the use he makes of their absence. For the role of an emotion or a relationship in a work of art, when that work is clearly a poetic and not a realistic fiction, is certainly not identical with its function or its value in life; and thus to judge it by the norm of "real life" implies that one has failed somehow in one's reading—or else that the artist himself has failed. The poet, by his very tone and language, means to release us (if we can hear him) from our conventional expectations. He means to make us feel external occurrences as representations of states of being. If he is a good poet he can make us grasp the nature of states which have no corresponding act or sign in the manifest living of life, and which *must therefore be rendered either by an invention of something quite new, or by a variation of something old.*

The latter is what Dante does in the love-story of the *Vita Nuova,* where the hero asks for nothing more in life than the lady's salutation. To take Dante to task, or to question his own virility because of this restriction in his tale, shows as pig-headed a literal-mindedness as to quarrel with *King Lear* because Lear's behaviour towards his daughters is an absurdity to common sense.[4] There is not the slightest hint in Dante's book that its hero-narrator refrains from desiring Beatrice through virtuous asceticism or masculine insufficiency. Indeed, although that would certainly have been a familiar and "conventional" enough romanticism, Dante's hero does not *refrain* from anything: he simply never takes the step from initial wonder and adoration to desire; and he does not take it because the story is trying to tell us something about that part of love

---

[4] But even this view has its practitioner in Leo Tolstoy, whose essay against *King Lear* deserves to be read by every serious student of literature.

which is not expressed or resolved in physical embraces. And this is the same part which very often attempts, and fails, to express itself in poetry; and frequently turns to prayer, or something which is the equivalent of prayer. In realistic terms the length of time Dante's hero spends in wonder and adoration might seem silly and unfortunate, as well as disproportionate. But that is beside the point. In the book, the time is right and real; in the book, it is true that love is, itself, the satisfaction of every desire it begets; and the beloved girl is a miracle, a *beatrice* (or blessing-bearer) who makes the whole world instantly luminous for her lover. And something of this intention must be felt before one is in a position to read Dante further to any purpose.

In an interim between the end of the *Vita Nuova's* story and the beginning of the *Comedy*—which is to say, between Beatrice's death and the hero's wanderings in the Dark Wood—the protagonist of both books has forgotten what Beatrice taught, and meshed himself in other loves. Yet he has not so completely forgotten her that she cannot rescue him. When the pilgrim is caught in the Dark Wood, it is she who comes to the edge of Hell, to despatch his rescuer; and it is her name and the promise that he will see her again that supply him with the courage he lacks to begin his journey. Virgil scatters reminders of Beatrice all along the difficult roads in Inferno and Purgatory; and he has perfect confidence in the virtue as well as the efficacy of making a lure of her. In one sort of reminder he assures the pilgrim that Beatrice will give him answers to those questions of his for which reason is an insufficient instrument. With another he heartens him to face perils: first, the entry into Hell; later, the passing through flames at the top of Purgatory, where "Now look, my son, twixt Beatrice and thee is this wall,"[5] melts the pilgrim's reluctance instantly.

So Beatrice's love, her wisdom and her presence are all employed as bait by the honest Virgil, to urge his pupil forward towards a goal which lies beyond Beatrice, but, as

[5] XXVII, 35–36

we shall see, is only to be reached through her. The wise
and reasonable Virgil, who knows how and how much he
is himself loved, knows also that Beatrice draws from his
pupil a different love, and is a key to understanding of a
totally different kind.

Such is the approach. But what Dante really wants to
say of Beatrice—what she is, over and above what the pilgrim feels her to be—we have scarcely begun to guess until
the angels of the divine pageant on the mountain top call
her forth in person. So important is that moment and the
scene which follows it, that we must have it before us in
detail.

1   *Quando il settentrion del primo cielo*
         che nè occaso mai seppe nè orto
         nè d'altra nebbia che di colpa velo,

       e che faceva lì ciascuno accorto
         di suo dover, come 'l più basso face
         qual temon gira per venire a porto,

       fermo s'affisse, la gente verace
         venuta prima tra 'l Grifone ed esso,
         al carro volse sè come a sua pace;

       e un di loro, quasi da ciel messo,
         "Veni, sponsa, de Libano" cantando
         gridò tre volte, a tutti li altri appresso.

       Quali i beati al novissimo bando
         surgeran presti ognun di sua caverna,
         la rivestita carne alleluiando;

       cotali in su la divina basterna
         si levar cento, ad vocem tanti senis,
         ministri e messaggier di vita etterna.

       Tutti dicean: "Benedictus qui venis!"
         e fior gittando di sopra e dintorno,
         "Manibus, o, date lilia plenis!"

       Io vidi già nel cominciar del giorno
         la parte orïental tutta rosata,
         e l'altro ciel di bel sereno adorno;

25   *e la faccia del sol nascere ombrata,*
         sì che, per temperanza di vapori,
         l'occhio la sostenea lunga fiata:

         così dentro una nuvola di fiori
         che dalle mani angeliche saliva
         e ricadeva in giù dentro e di fori,

         sovra candido vel cinta d'uliva
         donna m'apparve, sotto verde manto
33   *vestita di color di fiamma viva.*

When the wain of the first heaven which setting nor rising never knew, nor veil of other mist than of sin,

and which made there each one aware of his duty, even as the lower wain guides him who turns the helm to come into port,

had stopped still, the people of truth, who had first come between the grifon and it, turned then to the cart as to their peace;

and one of them as if sent from heaven "*Veni sponsa de Libano*" did shout thrice in song, and all the others after him.

As the saints at the last trump shall rise ready each one from his tomb, with re-clad voice singing Halleluiah,

such on the divine chariot rose up a hundred *ad vocem tanti senis*, ministers and messengers of life eternal.

All were saying "*Benedictus qui venis*"; and, strewing flowers above and around, "*Manibus, o, date lilia plenis.*"

Ere now have I seen, at dawn of day, the eastern part all rosy red, and the rest of heaven adorned with fair clear sky,

and the face of the sun rise shadowed, so that by the tempering of the mists, the eye long time endured him:

so within a cloud of flowers, which rose from the
angelic hands and fell down again within and without,

olive-crowned over a white veil, a lady appeared to
me, clad, under a green mantle, with hue of living
flame.

XXX, 1–33

This extraordinary invocation, spell-like, mysterious
however much explained, calls upon Beatrice in language
borrowed from the *Song of Songs*, where the speaker is,
literally, an impassioned lover; next it blesses her in words
taken with slight alteration from the Gospel of St Matthew, where *benedictus qui venit* is said of Jesus; and
finally it offers tributes of flowers in Anchises' words that
hail and praise the unborn hero, the youth Marcellus,
in the sixth book of the *Aeneid.* The very fact of such
quotation from hallowed texts in three urgent and hallow-
ing appeals, suggests that the event about to take place
here will have the sacred and timeless character of a mystery. She who is wished for will come, as did the glorious
Bride, as did Jesus, as did Marcellus. She will be for the
pilgrim his beloved, his saviour, and—in so far as he shall
re-create her in his poem—his offspring.

But here at once the absurdity of attempting to exhaust
the meaning of such a passage by a list of equivalences
becomes apparent. The words and their connotations com-
bine and recombine, and their sense far outreaches the
possibilities of a systematic reading, however irreproach-
able. The angelic words, Dante's own meltingly lyric analogy by which Beatrice is likened to the sun, and the simple
description of the lady according to her colours, which are
those of faith, hope and charity—all these prepare us for
a timeless, heaven-honoured wonder, and they serve as a
prelude to the rapture of recognition that follows when
the pilgrim, who cannot see Beatrice's face, knows her by
the trembling of his blood, waking the whole past:

E lo spirito mio che già cotanto
 tempo era stato che alla sua presenza
 non era di stupor, tremando, affranto,

sanza delli occhi aver più conoscenza,
 per occulta virtù che da lei mosse,
 d'antico amor sentì la gran potenza.

Tosto che nella vista mi percosse
 l'alta virtù che già m'avea trafitto
 prima ch'io fuor di puerizia fosse,

Volsimi alla sinistra . . .
. . . . . .

per dicere a Virgilio: "Men che dramma
 di sangue m'è rimaso che non tremi:
 conosco i segni dell'antica fiamma."

And my spirit, that now so long a time had passed
since, trembling in her presence, it had been broken
down with awe,

without having further knowledge by mine eyes,
through hidden virtue which went out from her, felt
the mighty power of ancient love.

Soon as on my sight the lofty virtue smote, which
already had pierced me ere I was out of my boyhood,

I turned me to the left . . .
. . . . . .

to say to Virgil: "Less than a drachm of blood is left
in me that trembleth not; I recognize the tokens of
the ancient flame."

         XXX, 34–48

Conosco i segni dell'antica fiamma: these are the words
that Virgil, in his own poem, put into the mouth of Queen
Dido, in recognition of a quite different resurgence of
love.[6] And they are bold and thrilling here, both because

[6] *Aeneid* IV, 23

they are like the unexpected quotation of a musical
theme, and because by their sense they remind us twice
over that the signs of all human loves are the same; the
blood will always tremble in rapture in the beloved presence, whether its desires are shaped by *Amor* or *Caritas*.

Each reader will notice with more or less of shock that
Beatrice does not answer in kind the pilgrim's flood of
emotion, in spite of the fact that its nature is necessarily
as clear to her as though he were made of crystal. She sees
him turn back to tell Virgil what has happened, and sees
the tears spring to his eyes when he finds Virgil gone.
Then she addresses him. Calling him by his given name—
here for the first time mentioned—she tells him to stop
weeping and listen to her, since she means to offer him a
far graver cause for tears than Virgil's departure. Her dis-
concerting sternness makes even the attendant angels compassionate. And by now any misapprehension which may
have led the reader to expect in Beatrice a tender Blessed
Damozel is bluntly corrected. Beatrice is stern because
she sees with terrible heavenly accuracy, and exercises her
power of truth without palliative or delay.

> *Guardaci ben! Ben son, ben son Beatrice.*
> *Come degnasti d'accedere al monte?*
> *non sapei tu che qui è l'uom felice?*
>
> *Li occhi mi cadder giù nel chiaro fonte;*
> *ma veggendomi in esso, i trassi all'erba,*
> *tanta vergogna mi gravò la fronte.*

"Look at me well; verily I am, verily I am Beatrice.
How didst thou deign to draw near the mount? knew-
est thou not that here man is happy?"

Mine eyes drooped down to the clear fount; but beholding me therein, I drew them back to the grass,
so great a shame weighed down my brow.

XXX, 73–78

The pilgrim turns from the mirroring water, but in this
moment Beatrice, too, is a mirror, and one he cannot

avoid. Her question ignores all that the climb through Purgatory has done to bring him out of the misery of the Dark Wood; it reflects him as he was when Virgil found him in the beast-ridden obscurity of the wood; and one gets the impression from the agony of his response that he now consciously sees this miserable image of himself for the first time. How did you deign to come here? she asks, and the question is bitter, but medicinal. The "ice which had closed about his heart" melts; he knows himself and Beatrice, and is enabled to make the confession which is at once recognition and penitence of personal error.

It is Beatrice who directs his thoughts to what he must here confess—not his sins of commission, but his insufficiently tenacious love of the good. Still stern and veiled, standing on the opposite bank of the stream among her handmaid Virtues, and witnessed by angels, she recalls her former, mortal beauty, the power of her "young eyes" to lead her lover "to the right goal", her death, and his defection in pursuit of "false visions of the good". In her living form he had been granted knowledge of a perfect human creature; thus in loving her he had loved the good, and knew well the difference between this and covetous or concupiscent loves. Still, when he could no longer see Beatrice, he had easily fallen away from the path she had shown him.

Now he acknowledges all her charges. It is a strange scene, painful and glorious, fusing elements it would seem impossible to join in poetry. Beatrice's speech is a "sword", well-aimed and sharp. She is a stern "admiral" and a harsh "mother", and "queenlike in bearing". Yet images of love dilate all through her merciless putting of the case.

> *Mai non t'appresentò natura o arte*
> *piacer, quanto le belle membra in ch'io*
> *rinchiusa fui, e sono in terra sparte;*
>
> *e se 'l sommo piacer sì ti fallìo*
> *per la mia morte, qual cosa mortale*
> *dovea poi trarre te nel suo disio?"*

"Ne'er did nature or art present to thee pleasure so great as the fair members wherein I was enclosed, and are scattered to dust;

and if the highest pleasure thus failed thee by my death, what mortal thing ought then to have drawn thee to desire it?"

XXXI, 49–53

Sotto 'l suo velo e oltre la rivera
vincer parìemi più sè stessa antica,
vincer che l'altre qui, quand'ella c'era.

Under her veil and beyond the stream she seemed to surpass more her ancient self than she surpassed the others here when she was with us.

XXXI, 82–84

The painful interrogation and the great beauty of the lady are harmonized in the strong, sweet flow of the lines; and Beatrice is easily as much mother as maiden and offended muse. What the lines of this whole passage describe has no bearing on the external events of the world, but belongs altogether to the internal, to the life of the spirit at its utmost intensity, where the approach to the essences of things no longer seems impossible. The miraculous encounter, which occurs literally in the Eden garden beside Lethe, does not show the pilgrim talking with a shadowy lady, or any sort of lady, but with a soul—a naked essence. And if we think what sort of essence, with what sort of hold over the pilgrim, what else could we expect except that it be infinitely alluring, and merciless in judgment?

It is in this part of the story that the image of Beatrice to be developed in the *Paradiso* begins to emerge. Here especially we must listen to and pause over the language, and take note without preconceptions of what the poem is making. Not that this will lead us to a "definition" of Beatrice, but that it will help us not to miss the purpose and power with which Dante maintains the pilgrim's love-rapture within the framework of their altered relationship

—his ignorance and humbleness, and her transcendent wisdom.

When Beatrice's eyes are revealed, we are reminded by the Virtues, her handmaids, that these are the very eyes of the young Beatrice:

> *"posto t'avem dinanzi alli smeraldi*
> *ond'Amor già ti trasse le sue armi."*

"we have placed thee before the emeralds whence Love once drew his shafts at thee."

XXXI, 116

"A thousand desires hotter than flame" hold the pilgrim bound to these eyes, but what he now sees in them shows them to be the eyes of the *new* Beatrice: the Christ-grifon at which she is gazing is reflected in her eyes not in its external single shape, but with the attributes successively of its human and of its divine nature. Thus the reflection is not a physical image of the creature, but, as it were, a metaphysical one. Beatrice's eyes, we infer, mirror the internalized, the *understood* form of what she sees. This is the first wonder she performs, and it is significant with respect to all the others. Her eyes reflect divine truths; her face is lit by the "glory of living light eternal".

What sort of lady is this, we may well ask; and what do such powers mean? There is a passage in Thomas Aquinas which gives some light on this:

> Now rightness of judgment may come about in two ways: the first resulting from perfect use of reason: the second from a certain connaturalness with the things being judged. . . . Accordingly, to judge rightly about divine things after rational inquiry pertains to that wisdom which is an intellectual virtue: but to judge rightly about them through connaturalness with them pertains to that wisdom which is a gift of the Holy Spirit.[7]

[7] Thomas Aquinas, *Summa Theologica*, II, II, xlv. I am indebted to J. B. Fletcher, *Symbolism of the Divine Comedy*, for pointing out the relevance of this passage.

Beatrice possesses both sorts of right judgment. She rebukes the pilgrim and confesses him according to the "perfect use of reason"; but the whole episode of the invocation and the unveiling of her eyes suggests "a certain connaturalness" with Christ, yielding another sort of wisdom, direct and unreasoned. And this will be borne out by her teaching throughout the remainder of the pilgrim's journey. One might add that if the pilgrim can receive her teachings it is because he loves her; and that everything about the sudden and spontaneous love narrated in the *Vita Nuova* indicates, as one looks back on it, a certain connaturalness making her known to him at the instant of their first meeting.

I speak still of the literal Beatrice—of a transfigured human soul, and not of her allegorical significance. But the scene we have been discussing, and the further events in the Garden, press home the sense of an unfolding symbolism of the sort to which Dante gave the name of allegory,[8] and we are ready now to examine an interpretation which maintains the integrity and primacy of the literal image.

Charles Singleton in his essay, "The Pattern at the Center"[9] has made plain both the substance and the importance of the analogy between Beatrice and Christ which is so insistently suggested in the *Vita Nuova*. He has shown that this analogy as it emerges again in the scene before us—the portentous return of Beatrice to the lover whom she had in her first life drawn towards a vision of the good—has as its purpose to forecast the second coming of Christ.

This insight opens up a new depth in our understanding of Beatrice's role. And it gives the scene with which we have been concerned a new depth of ritual solemnity; for, in a certain sense, Beatrice's appearance solicits Christ to

[8] Standard "allegory" is a fiction of a quite different sort: one in which the literal characters have no (or little) interest apart from what they signify.

[9] C. Singleton, *Commedia: Elements of Structure* (Harvard Univ. Press, 1954)

fulfil his promised action in mercy and love, as she performs hers. In the allegory of the *Comedy* the protagonist is mankind; and in the Garden scene it is mankind-as-it-ought-to-be—penitent and regenerate. The action in this scene is the meeting of mankind with Christ in his second coming: Christ as he *may* be—loving and stern. In the allegory, then, Beatrice signifies Christ. It will be noted that the terms of her literal existence in Dante's two books are not laid aside in the pointing of this signification, but are drawn upon fully: for both Beatrice and Christ lived in the world and opened certain eyes to a new conception of love; both died and were transfigured in heaven; one, at this point in the *Comedy*, comes to the rescue of the lover who has wandered from her teaching; the other is still expected by all the faithful. Furthermore the literal Beatrice does not vanish, is not obscured, to make this meaning possible, but remains in the foreground of stage and thought, fulfilling in this, her second coming, the promise of her first: her beauty now fully revealed, she is friend, teacher and guide to the particular human pilgrim to whom she now gives his particular human name, Dante, in sign of his attained manhood. We might say that the allegory *arises from* Beatrice, and not only does not diminish her, but enriches our conception of her. She remains the Lady of the *Comedy*; her revealed spirit, the divine principle in her, is never for a moment cut off from its fair, familiar, limited identity.

II

There was a road to pursue in Inferno, a bitter and difficult descent from circle to circle, along which Virgil showed the pilgrim where and how to set his feet, carrying him bodily for whole stretches where the peril was great. Purgatory was a concrete mountain to be climbed; and again Virgil, following the sun, and occasionally enquiring the way of those better acquainted with the place, showed the direction, encouraging, prodding and coaxing his pupil to follow. In Paradise there is no road. The spaces between the planetary heavens are traversed effortlessly, and remain virtually imperceptible to the pilgrim, while the planets themselves are pathless and without landscape—stages of spiritual initiation rather than places. The pilgrim, moreover, now that he has passed the tests and received the blessings of the Terrestrial Paradise, is so "without impediment" that heavenward motion is second nature to him. Says Beatrice:

> "*ma folgore, fuggendo il proprio sito,*
> *non corse come tu ch'ad esso riedi.*"

"lightning, fleeing its proper site, ne'er darted as dost thou who art returning thither."

Par. I, 92–93

and

> "*Non dei più ammirar, se bene stimo*
> *lo tuo salir, se non come d'un rivo*
> *se d'alto monte scende giuso ad imo.*"

"Thou shouldst no more wonder . . . at thine uprising than at a river dropping down from a lofty mountain to the base."

I, 136–138

Thus Beatrice does not guide along the physical route as Virgil did. She accompanies; and she teaches things which make the pilgrim of his own freshly acquired power rise towards further insights. She has two ways of teaching: by the sheer radiance of her face (especially her eyes, in which her wisdom is self-evident), and by her speech, in which intuitive knowledge is translated into rational discourse for her companion's sake.

The unveiling scene in the Terrestrial Paradise taught us some things about the powers of Beatrice's countenance: the *thousand desires* begotten by her emerald eyes, the *ancient net* snaring her lover again, the divine radiance. The opening narrative of the *Paradiso* reveals still further powers. Standing with the pilgrim alone in the Garden when all the rituals have been completed, Beatrice gazes at the sun in the noonday sky. The pilgrim, unable to bear the direct blaze of its light, transfers his gaze to her

eyes and feels their content poured over into him. At
once he knows himself transmuted in a way which he can
only hint through the analogy of a myth:

> *Nel suo aspetto tal dentro mi fei,*
>   *qual si fè Glauco nel gustar dell'erba*
>   *che'l fè consorte in mar delli altri Dei.*
>
> *Trasumanar significar per verba*
>   *non si porìa; però l'essemplo basti*
>   *a cui esperïenza grazia serba.*

Gazing on her such I became as was Glaucus, tasting
of the grass that made him the seafellow of the other
Gods.

To pass beyond humanity may not be told in words,
wherefore let the example satisfy him for whom grace
reserveth the experience.

I, 67–72

The verb *trasumanar* may be rendered literally as *trans-
humanize*. We surmise from it that the pilgrim has become Beatrice's heavenfellow; that he is now "connatural"
with her. He does not say so, but humbly thanks "love
who rulest heaven" and who "with thy light didst lift me
up".[10]

Beatrice's eyes, then, look at the sun and reflect, not
physical light but intellectual light, pure, simple, direct
and formless. We are prepared by her wonderful eyeing
of the grifon for this translation of things into their
truths. The pilgrim has not yet her power, but his transhumanization has made him her perfect understudy. As
she is suffused with sunlight, entering her directly as in-
tuition of God (for so we must infer from her instant

[10] It is interesting that the pilgrim should here thank, not
Beatrice, but "love who rulest heaven". This *amor* is of course
clearly God, and neither a pagan godling nor the charming hypos-
tasis of the *Vita Nuova*. And there is no offence in naming God
according to some one of the qualities of his being, for the prac-
tice had Thomas Aquinas' sanction. But the effect of this *amor*
is nonetheless quite as though it *were* addressed to Beatrice "who
rulest heaven"—so that even after we have made the proper sense
of it, it binds Beatrice to God by one more thread.

rising upward into a sphere closer to the Truth), so the
pilgrim is suffused with light reflected from her eyes,
causing him also to rise at her side. His eyes, like Glaucus'
senses, are equipped for new perceptions.

Light continues to stream from Beatrice's eyes into the
pilgrim's as the two rise upward on the first stage of the
journey into the *deiform realm*—the one borne by newly
freed instinct towards his *proper site*; the other, whose
instinct has long been perfect, now released from the
weight of her lover's misapprehension, which drew her
down to serve him. As they progress into heavenly things,
Beatrice's image increases in splendour, and combines attributes no lady ever united before. She is at once brilliant, holy, wise and bewitching. She is a prism filled with
divine light and an acute dispenser of that light, capable
of manifesting its smallest mote in discursive language.
At the same time the old spell of her beauty, far from
shrinking in this high place, increases at every upward
step.

To be sure, not all the odd harmonies in the poetry
Dante composes about her were of his invention. The
mingling of the languages of erotic and sacred love in
much of the prose and poetry devoted to the Virgin Mary
must have been as familiar to Dante as to his readers.
But the combination of the erotic with the purely intellectual—that, I suppose, was his own daring innovation,
and probably bears his copyright to this day without even
a single attempt to infringe.

This brings us to the vexed question of Beatrice's second way of teaching—those discourses, scattered throughout the *Paradiso*, which regularly make large numbers of
readers restive and impudent. The cause of their disquiet
is easier to define than remedy. They feel both that Beatrice talks excessively and that they are themselves the
target of her difficult lessons. They are perhaps not altogether wrong in assuming that Dante would have wished
them to absorb Beatrice's teaching—but that whole question is quite beside the point artistically, since the success
of the poem does not in any way hinge upon what he may

have wished. The real problem that the discourses present is not that they are extraneous (which they are not), or that they are aimed at the reader (which we do not know), but that they are difficult, and that the reader must drudge over them until he knows their drift—whereupon they will fall back from their painful prominence into their proper place as a portion of the felt content of the poem. This they may be counted upon to do, for they are in no sense detached embellishments, but are an utterly necessary portion of the story—a series of intellectual keys necessary to its particular heaven-viewing protagonist, with his rational, discursive mind. They are the intellectual counterpart of the increasing light visible in Beatrice's eyes as she rises from heaven to heaven. But they are also poetically necessary—the very armature of the visible images of Paradise, without which the light itself would collapse in the reader's imagination like a gauze scarf falling.

Nor do Beatrice's lectures cancel out the magical and silent attraction of her eyes, which only increase their hold over the pilgrim as they come closer to the source of light. It is Dante's intention to maintain unbroken within the atmosphere of these discourses the pilgrim's rapturous *élan*. And such is the force of his conviction, that the reader who does not allow himself to be sidetracked by the discourses (that is to say, by his intellectual concern with them) feels this extraordinary combination as one thing, absolutely new in poetry as it is new in the qualification of Heaven. The poet deliberately entwines the terminology of love with that of scholastic argument. He says of Beatrice:

> *Quel sol che pria d'amor mi scaldò 'l petto,*
> *di bella verità m'avea scoverto,*
> *provando e riprovando, il dolce aspetto;*

That sun which first warmed my bosom with love, had thus unveiled for me by proof and refutation fair truth's sweet aspect.

III, 1–3

If these lines somewhat startle, they nonetheless give us a sharp sense of the revision of romantic love which the poet has already achieved. We see how he means to demonstrate in this beloved figure, whose gentleness and silence were in the *Vita Nuova* constant instruments of her power, that truth of every sort is compatible with—or even inseparable from—beauty. It is for this reason that he sets out, not without a certain captivating audacity, to make even *proof* and *refutation* winsome. They belong to the province of intellectual light, which is Paradise; they are its *persuasions*. Truth appears in Beatrice's eyes, simple and whole, under the image of imbibed light; her mouth utters it in analysis, providing those explanations which are still necessary to the pilgrim's querying intellect; and there is no real discrepancy between the two sorts of teaching, for the one flows from the other[11] and both flow from the primal Truth through Beatrice. Thus we read following one of her speeches:

> Cotal fu l'ondeggiar del santo rio
>   ch'uscì del fonte ond'ogni ver deriva;
>   tal puose in pace uno e altro disio.

> "O amanza del primo amante, o diva"
>   diss'io appresso "il cui parlar m'inonda
>   e scalda sì, che più e più m'avviva,

> non è l'affezïon mia sì profonda,
>   che basti a render voi grazia per grazia.

Such the rippling of the sacred stream which issued from the Spring whence all truth downfloweth; and being such, it set at peace one and the other longing.

"O love of the primal Lover, O divine one," said I then, "whose speech o'erfloweth me and warmeth, so that more and more it quickeneth me,

my love hath no such depth as to suffice to render grace for grace."

IV, 115–122

[11] As the whole manifest world flows from the primal unity of the godhead.

The rippling of the stream is Beatrice's voice and her statement; the stream is the whole vein of truth flowing concomitantly with love into the universe, to be caught up in such channels as Beatrice, and witnessed by the intent mind that seeks for it.

But the gift of Beatrice to her lover is not her arguments and conclusions. When she says: "Thee . . . stripped in thine intellect would I inform with light so living it shall tremble as thou lookest on it,"[12] she makes it perfectly plain that the piecemeal lessons are nothing more than a means to the end of undivided light. And this is what she means, and what all her arguments result in: enlightenment. Now there is no breach of pure romantic ardour in this image of living light which connects Beatrice with God and the pilgrim with Beatrice, and will persist throughout the poem. Romantic love has always found its lady angelic, radiant, capable of awakening all the higher faculties, worthy of adoration. But romantic love does not examine the ground for this form of alerted exultancy—and Dante does. And he establishes the ground by making her *literally* a channel of divine things and literally able to set right for him the very premises of his moral existence.

With each further teaching as with each rising from planet to planet, Beatrice is seen as more beautiful. When the two ascend into Venus:

> Io non m'accorsi del salire in ella;
> ma d'esservi entro mi fè assai fede
> la donna mia ch' i' vidi far più bella.

I had no sense of rising into her, but my lady gave me full faith that I was there, because I saw her grow more beautiful.

VIII, 13–15

Entering into Mars:

> Ma Beatrice sì bella e ridente
> mi si mostrò, che tra quelle vedute
> si vuol lasciar che non seguir la mente.

12 *Par*. II, 109–11

Beatrice showed herself to me so beauteous and smiling, it must be left among the sights that followed
not my memory.

XIV, 79–81

Reaching Jupiter:

> Io mi rivolsi . . .
> per vedere in Beatrice il mio dovere
>
> .   .   .   .   .
>
> e vidi le sue luci tanto mere,
> tanto giooonde, che la sua sembianza
> vinceva li altri e l'ultimo solere.

I turned . . . to see in Beatrice my duty . . .

and I saw her eyes so clear, so joyous, that her semblance surpassed all former usage.

XVIII, 52–57

All the charm of these increases in beauty, mounting
until finally the poet lacks words altogether to express what
he sees, is rooted—as all Dante's charms are—in the growth
of the central and serious image. What we are to understand is that we are in the presence of the human intelligence as we all dream of it—perfectly awake and perfectly
floodlit, without any impediment between it and its object, and with its object maintained always in true perspective. To be sure, the other members of Heaven enjoy
unimpeded vision: all of them see contingent things in
their relation to absolutes, and eternal things as portions
of the One. And much of what the pilgrim learns is taught
him by these others. But Beatrice is more than the best
of eyes; she is the personality of the beloved, through
whom he sees so well, and through whom he is led to ask
his questions. So that it is in her that the gradual inte-
gration of his understanding takes place. He draws it whole
from her eyes, and piecemeal but harmonious from her
speech.

There has been no break in the love-story; but if we
look back now to its beginnings, which held all this in

germ, the elevation it has reached is dizzying. Beatrice is the same in soul as she was in body—only more translucent and far closer to the source of light. Earlier she suggested divine things; now she makes them manifest. Her beauty is uniquely a reflection of her spiritual being. The pilgrim loves her more with each increase of her beauty because with each he sees more clearly what she is. The poet would have us generalize from the increasing beauty, that this is the way with every truth-bearing created thing as we perceive it more and more fully. Similarly, the spectator's love (and this he tells us explicitly), if it is directed to the essential "form" of things and not to their "accidental" or external qualities, derives from understanding, and grows in proportion with it:

> E dei saper che tutti hanno diletto
> quanto la sua veduta si profonda
> nel vero in che si queta ogni intelletto.

> Quinci si può veder come si fonda
> l'esser beato nell'atto che vede,
> non in quel ch'ama, che poscia seconda.

And thou shouldst know that all have their delight in measure as their sight sinketh more deep into the truth wherein every intellect is stilled.

Hence may be seen that the being blessed is founded on the act that seeth, not that which loveth, which after followeth.

XXVIII, 106–111[13]

There is one more marvel in the image of Beatrice that sets her off from the other inhabitants of Heaven. She resembles, except for her greater translucence and beauty, the living Beatrice.

Souls in Purgatory were still close enough to the world of differentiation to be wearing shadowy semblances of their former bodies. In Paradise, however, the elect appear all along the way in forms accurately expressive of their

[13] See also XXIX, 139 and XXXIII, 92–93

new condition. In the Moon, the aerial bodies are still visible, grown far more tenuous; in Mercury featureless "splendours" greet the pilgrim; and from here on through the Primo Mobile, burning sparks of light whose individuality lies entirely in their speech. In the Empyrean all the souls reappear as jewelled blossoms beside a river bank, where Beatrice declares that they are as yet merely "the shadowy prefaces of their reality". Finally, "as folk under masks seem other than before if they do off the semblance not their own wherein they hid them", the elect undergo a change which makes them once again visible in their individual features. Each of these successive appearances, we are told, is truer than the preceding one; and yet each, except the last, is a symbolic mask. We are left to infer that the perfected eyes of the pilgrim, having now learned what each symbol-mask had to teach him, are no longer capable of being deluded by what is delusive in the human form.

But Beatrice! Beatrice, since her eyes were first unveiled to him in the Terrestrial Paradise has shown the pilgrim the same face and body. And these we know from his recognition of them were perfect copies of her living looks. So that what he sees when he looks at her in the Celestial Rose of the uppermost Heaven is, we may suppose, almost exactly (save for the really inconsequential changes of her added years) what the *Vita Nuova* says he saw when they met as young children, and when

> I say most truly that the spirit of life which hath its dwelling in the secretest chamber of the heart, began to tremble so violently that the least pulses of my body shook therewith; and in trembling it said these words: "Here is a deity stronger than I; who, coming, shall rule over me."[14]

We must conjecture what Dante meant by this changelessness of Beatrice in Heaven, for he neither explains it nor calls our attention to it except as the continuous awareness of her eyes and her smile may do so. If we reverse our

[14] *Vita Nuova* II, tr. by D. G. Rossetti

question and ask first why the other souls of the elect appear as sparks of light, we may come to understand Beatrice. For we see that the souls as brightnesses are able to reveal the essential principle of their being, free from any blurring it may have undergone in its physical embodiment. In the thirteenth canto of the *Paradiso* we are permitted to hear St Thomas discoursing on such blurrings. In created things, he says, matter and ideal form are never in perfect harmony, because Nature's hand is tremulous and cannot exactly match the mould she furnishes to the informing idea as it comes from God.[15] The elect, then, as they reveal themselves for the pilgrim's benefit, from the heaven of Mercury through that of Saturn, part temporarily with all visible evidence of their identity in order to make clear to him the nature of the life-giving principle. That a similar change is unnecessary in Beatrice suggests that the pilgrim, by the power of love, had from the beginning seen her without error.

That is one interpretation; and it suits well our speculation from our chief base in the literal story. But there is another which leads into the allegory. Dante's St Thomas tells us that Adam and Christ, moulded by God's hand instead of Nature's, were perfectly embodied souls, supremely endowed with light; and "human nature never was nor shall be such as in those two persons".[16] Beatrice is no exception to this prophetic dictum. But because both her endowment and the perfection of its embodiment were extraordinarily great, there is no need for her to change her human semblance in any of the revealing heavens. Like Christ, whom she typifies throughout the allegory, she had come into the world as a "miracle" of luminous wisdom and love, whose message could have been read correctly by any man with clear and ready eyes. The pilgrim, as we have seen, did read her correctly. Thus in Paradise, having come full circle from the purity of the child's vision, through blindness and recovery, to the purity of the transcendent vision, *knowing* finally what he

15 XIII, 55 ff.   16 XIII, 86–87

had at first divined and subsequently forgotten, he sees
no change in Beatrice other than increase of beauty.

This is not all Dante means. The changeless appearance
of Beatrice serves also as a praise of life. Death, according
to Dante's understanding, is not a blotting out but a free-
ing of the individual essence from all that may have
clouded it in life. Thus the beauty perceived in Heaven
is not new-made, but rather new-revealed to the spectator
in a process which regenerates the eyes by redefining the
object. In Beatrice's case alone there is no apparent change
—both because the pilgrim had always seen her correctly,
under the incentive of love, and because in her there had
never been any discord between appearance and reality. In
both senses, the poem announces through Beatrice what
Dante feels with such an energy of exaltation that the
whole poem stirs with it: that an earthly thing may be perfect, and that it may be experienced in its perfection. And
thus it expresses his ingrained sense of the world's redemption. The Son of God was indeed the Son of Man. Flesh
and the pure light are not inimical. And although Dante
perceives the light to be more often than not blurred in the
human creature, he knows it is there, capable of being
apprehended and loved, capable of irradiating the obscurity of pilgrim eyes, and thus of leading towards God.

All this means in addition that the view conventionally
associated with mediaeval thought, which regards the body
as a dark prison and its invitations as a source of frenzy,
is not to be found in Dante. His story, like his belief,
runs altogether counter to the pagan current in mediaeval
thought which Denis de Rougemont stresses in his study
of the Tristan legend with its philtre-drunk lovers groping
blindly for one another's arms, seeking annihilation.[17] But
if this serener view of Dante's is in harmony with the
Christian teaching, it seems nonetheless to be rooted below the level of reason in Dante's feeling, and to wrestle
at every turn of the poem with the pessimism which his
experience of life engenders. A perpetual dialogue between
the elements of delight and hope and those of despair in

[17] D. de Rougemont, *L'Amour et L'Occident* (Paris 1939)

the living world is one of the inexhaustible energies of the poem. It is a real, not a formal and prejudged dialogue, because both its hope and its despair had vigorous holds in the mind that composed the *Comedy*. The beginning of the *Inferno* makes it clear that Dante knew the pull of the dark, annihilating desire in more of its forms than the Tristan authors did. And his protagonist, trapped in the Dark Wood, swooning before Francesca, catching angry fire from Farinata, stunned into silence by Piero della Vigna, coiling Bocca degli Abati's hair round his fist, knows it, too, in various forms. But pliant human desire and not the unalterable human condition are responsible for such plights. Dante is aware that the whole world is off course, "beating its wings downward" in a general struggle of greed to possess its loves; and of himself, at times, caught in the same rush. And still his ingrained sense of life is totally opposed to the "pagan" sense, with its disparagement of the miserable, blind body. Dante *feels* the presence of light—sometimes bright, sometimes very murky indeed—in the world's creatures. Which is to say that he loves them spontaneously and cannot, on deliberation, refuse validity to that love. He loves them; he knows the dangers of love; he finds the cure in the replacement of desire by the exalted stasis of recognition. The mind and its knowledge are the answer to the body, and are the final goal of human life. Action is for speculation's sake; for speculation, as says the *De Monarchia* is "the supreme function for which the Prime Excellence brought the human race into being."[18]

Thus Dante can, in the one poem, acknowledge Hell and show us Beatrice quenching desire in the flood of joyous recognition she arouses. And his protagonist, safely beyond the "shadow" and "poison" of the flesh, can say to St John, questioning him on his love for God:

> *"Tutti quei morsi*
> *che posson far lo cor volgere a Dio,*
> *alla mia caritate son concorsi;*

[18] *De Mon.* I, iii

chè l'essere del mondo e l'esser mio,
la morte oh'el sostenne perch'io viva,
e quel che spera ogni fedel com'io,

con la predetta conoscenza viva,
tratto m'hanno del mar dell'amor torto,
e del diritto m'han posto alla riva.

Le fronde onde s'infronda tutto l'orto
dell'ortolano etterno, am'io cotanto
quanto da lui a lor di bene è porto."

"All those toothgrips which have power to make the heart turn unto God, co-work upon my love;

for the being of the world and my own being, the death that he sustained that I might live, and that which each believer hopeth, as do I,

together with the aforesaid living consciousness, have drawn me from the sea of the perverted and placed me on the shore of the right love.

The leaves wherewith all the garden of the eternal Gardener is leafed, I love in measure of the good that hath been proffered to them from him."

XXVI, 55–66

Chapter V

ASPECTS OF MINOR IMAGERY

(a) METAPHOR AND COMPARISON

Writing on Dante's imagery, T. S. Eliot says:

"Dante's attempt is to make us see what he saw. He therefore employs very simple language and very few metaphors, for allegory and metaphor do not get on well together. And there is a peculiarity about his *comparisons* which is worth noting in passing.

"There is a well-known comparison in the great XVth canto of the Inferno, which Matthew Arnold singled out, rightly, for high praise; which is characteristic of the way in which Dante employs these figures. He is speaking of the crowd in Hell who peered at him and his guide under a dim light:

> *e sì ver noi aguzzavan le ciglia,*
> *come vecchio sartor fa nella cruna . . .*

and sharpened their vision (knitted their brows) at us, like an old tailor at the eye of his needle.

"The purpose of this type of simile is solely to make us see *more definitely* the scene which Dante has put before us in the preceding lines.

> *She looks like sleep,*
> *As she would catch another Antony*
> *In her strong toil of grace.*

"The image of Shakespeare's is much more complicated than Dante's, and more complicated than it looks. It has the grammatical form of a kind of simile (the 'as if' form), but of course 'catch in her toil' is a metaphor. But whereas the simile of Dante is merely to make you see more clearly how the people looked, and is explanatory, the figure of Shakespeare is expansive rather than intensive; its purpose is to add to what you see (either on the stage or in your imagination) a reminder of that fascination of Cleopatra which shaped her history and that of the world, and of that fascination being so strong that it prevails even in death."[1]

This excerpt from the celebrated essay on Dante sheds a strong beam of light on the *Inferno*, but must puzzle the reader who tries to apply its observations generally to the *Comedy*. They seem inadequate to one's *experience* of the poem—which suggests a more various and malleable imagery. And on inspection, they fall short of the facts.

The metaphors of the *Inferno* are indeed few, and its similes largely designed "to make us see more definitely the scene", but the *Purgatorio* is quite another story. Not only are the *Purgatorio's* metaphors numerous but in the majority of them visual clarity and interpretive insight are there together (with a marked purpose of "adding to what you see"), while in a few (the most striking), visible likeness drops away in favour of insight. As for the *Paradiso*, its discourse glitters with metaphors that say nothing of any visible scene whatever.

If one further studies these images in their setting along the course of the poem, one comes to feel sure that something more interesting than the individual bent of the Alighieri eyes, and more powerful than literary tradition or literary innovation, is at work here. The imagery is not predominantly of one kind, nor is it a bouquet. Rather, it varies and develops, in close and revealing correspondence with the growth of the pilgrim protagonist; and not by conscious plan, but by action of a poetic imagination

[1] Eliot, T. S.: "Dante" in *Selected Essays* (Harcourt, Brace, New York, 1932), p. 205 and (Faber and Faber, London, 3rd Edition 1951), pp. 243-44.

which responds *wholly* to the quality of each successive moment of experience. In other words, the imagery of metaphor and analogy reflects the growth of the pilgrim's understanding in his progress from the Dark Wood of spiritual blindness, through gradual acquisitions of insight into universal order, to the point where he can not only "read" all the scattered pages of the "book" of the universe, but can see in a single glance the whole restored. What follows here is an attempt to substantiate this conclusion.

Inferno

In the first canticle the principle images are explicit comparisons (similes and analogies), and the principal comparisons show us exactly what things looked like—not because it was the poet's purpose "to make us see more definitely the scene" which he had put before us, but *because to see the scene was precisely all the pilgrim in his condition of mortal ignorance could do*.[2] A narrowly escaped candidate for permanent residence in Hell, he could see no deeper into the scene than the sensuous qualities by which one thing may seem to resemble another. For this reason in Inferno the meanings of things are in abeyance (the pilgrim being unable to detect them, the poet cannot overtly express them), and sensuous detail is predominantly sharp. One might say that the quality of Dante's comparisons shows us, not the nature of his poetic imagination absolutely, as Mr Eliot suggests, but the nature of that imagination working within the peculiar experience of Hell.

The clear comparisons of the *Inferno* render nothing but what the senses might record from present or past scenes: the furniture and actions of Hell and of remembered earth. But, although the pilgrim's view (to which the poet is always faithful) is thus limited, the very fact that what he had before him was a stage of *souls laid bare*

---

[2] I am indebted to an early lecture by Francis Fergusson for observations which suggested this train of thought with regard to the action of the *Inferno*.

would seem to promise that even the simplest tangible
aspects of that world must offer clues to its meaning. *The
clues were there; they are rendered in the poem.* Because
they could not be read by the pilgrim when he saw them,
Dante transcribes them without stress, hidden in the ap-
parently sufficient concrete comparisons. And because they
are hidden they may easily be missed by the reader; no
poet ever more grandly took that risk.

The comparison quoted by Mr Eliot is one such silent
clue-bearer. It describes the first meeting of Dante and
Virgil with the Sodomites in the darkness of their fiery
circle. I quote it together with the twin comparison that
immediately precedes it:

> *e ciascuna*
> *ci riguardava come suol da sera*
>
> *guardare uno altro sotto nuova luna;*
> *e sì ver noi aguzzavan le ciglia*
> *come 'l vecchio sartor fa ne la cruna.*

and each looked hard at us as people do to see

> each other at evening under a new moon; and they
> sharpened their brows towards us like an old tailor
> at his needle's eye.[3]

> XV, 17–21

Taken by itself this passage with its two arresting comparisons seems intended simply to delineate exactly the
striving glance of the sinners—a glance such as might occur
anywhere where light is poor and the object to be viewed
somewhat unfamiliar. But it matters that this glance does
not occur just anywhere: it happens precisely in Hell,
where poorness of light and weakness of eyes are conditions
of the soul; and, more particularly, it is the glance of the
Sodomites—lovers who make a wrong identification of
love's object. The pair of images that describes their glance
at Dante and Virgil reflects something of their mode of
being: a restless, eager, personal curiosity about the new-

[3] The translations in this section of chapter V are the author's.

comer, whoever he may be. This moonlight, squint-eyed glance is our introduction to these souls: it "adds to what we see" a preparation in feeling for the close and somewhat ambiguous personal encounter which is to follow between the pilgrim and Brunetto Latini. It "expands" the mere facts of the scene before the reader's eye.

In many other images of the *Inferno* (those especially in the favoured form of analogy) one finds an expansion of similar sort. The poet whose pictures grasp the mind so strongly seldom sees merely picturesquely, and *never* describes anything for the sake of an isolated impression. The wonder of the poem is not its multifold attractions so much as its almost incredible integrity, never broken by failure of meaning or by meaning disconnected from the great divine and moral explanation of the cosmos.

The bird images of Canto V (which concerns those who "subject reason to lust") are not merely appropriate to the windy scene and the graceful crowding shapes of the sinners: they recall that perfection of instinctual living to which the lovers of the second Circle—forgetting that they were creatures of reason no less than of nature—aspired. For a moment the unguarded reader, falling into Hell along with the pilgrim, thinks *ah yes, of course they are like swift starlings, like singing cranes, like tender doves— poor helpless loving things, so pitiful in the merciless wind.* But he is expected to come to his senses and to realize that the tempest, which is an unavoidable accident in the life of starlings, was the choice of those human souls.

Of the itching, scratching falsifiers, who lean against one another like warming pans, we read:

> e sì traevan giù l'unghie la scabbia,
> come coltel di scardova le scaglie
> o d'altro pesce che più larghe l'abbia.

and so their nails scraped off the scabs as a knife scrapes the scales from bream or other fish that has them larger.

XXIX, 82–84

We are in the deepest ditch of the eighth Circle, almost as far from the life-supporting sun as one can get, almost in the icy centre of spiritual death. The two scratchers, Griffolino and Capocchio, are seen in an image which shows us exactly what their gestures looked like, and at the same time tells us metaphorically the nature of their plight: their bodies like pans, their hands like scaling-knives, their flesh like bream or carp, humanity is utterly blighted in them; a nervous compulsion is all that animates them: the twitch of deliberate greed. As the passage develops, the images generate the horror of dehumanization—a horror curiously enhanced when Virgil, ever impeccable in honesty, addresses one of these souls as

> "O tu che con le dita ti dismaglie,
>
> . . . . .
>
> e che fai d'esse tal volta tanaglie,
> dinne . . ."

Oh you who use your fingers to dismail yourself, . . .
sometimes making them into pincers,

tell us . . .   XXIX, 85–88

The major images of *Inferno* are of this kind: sharp visual comparisons with powerful metaphorical overtones. But there is another group in which the overtone of the visual works in a different way. In Canto XV, 4–12, as the pilgrim enters the circle of the Violent against Nature, we read:

> Quale i Fiamminghi tra Guizzante e Bruggia,
>   temendo il fiotto che 'nver lor s'avventa,
>   fanno lo schermo perchè 'l mar si fuggia;
>
> e quale i Padovan lungo la Brenta,
>   per difender lor ville e lor castelli,
>   anzi che Chiarentana il caldo senta;
>
> a tale imagine eran fatti quelli,
>   tutto che nè sì alti nè sì grossi,
>   qual che si fosse, lo maestro felli.

As the Flemish between Wissant and Bruges fearing
the waters that come rushing toward them, build up
their dikes to put the sea to flight;

and as the Paduans do along the Brenta to make their
villages and castles safe before Carinthia feels the
heat:

so had the builder of those banks, whoever he might
be, devised them, though not so thick and not so
great in height.

The ideal reader may be supposed to know the purpose
of a Flemish dike and what it looks like, and to be familiar
with the flood-barriers of Padua in Dante's time. He can,
then, visualize the high banks of the crimson stream that
give Virgil and the pilgrim safe foot-passage across the
burning sands. But need he be reminded by *two* examples?
By Padua as well as Flanders? And with a mysterious allusion to the maker of the infernal bulwarks thrown in?
Surely not if *to see the scene* was all that was required.
But there is something else that issues from this passage:
an implicit affirmation of contrast—a forcible reminder, in
the very vitality of purpose at Bruges and Padua, of the
deadness of this infernal habitation and of the unnatural-
ness of its geography (the destructive fire replacing the
life-giving waters of earth); and finally of the fact that
the "citizens" here did not choose and do not know the
architect of *their* dike.

In Canto XXI, 7–18, a similar analogy describes the
river of pitch in which are steeped those who bought and
sold public offices.

> *Quale nell 'arzanà de' Viniziani*
> *bolle l'inverno la tenace pece*
> *a rimpalmare i legni lor non sani,*
>
> *chè navicar non ponno; in quella vece*
> *chi fa suo legno novo e chi ristoppa*
> *le coste a quel che più viaggi fece;*

chi ribatte da proda e chi da poppa;
altri fa remi e altri volge sarte;
chi terzeruolo e artimon rintoppa;

tal, non per foco, ma per divin' arte,
bollìa là giuso una pegola spessa,
che 'nviscava la ripa d'ogni parte.

As in the arsenal of the Venetians the sticky pitch
boils in the winter months to caulk the damaged ships

that cannot put to sea; instead one man rebuilds his
ship, another stops the ribs of his that has made many
voyages;

some hammer at a prow and some at stern; others
make oars or mend the ropes; some patch a mainsail
or a jib;

so, not by fire, but by divine art a thick pitch boiled
down there below, and on all sides beglued the banks.

All that is actually compared here is the boiling pitch of
Venetian arsenal and of infernal river. But that marvellous
activity of seagoing preparation that lies between the two
terms of the comparison, and which might at first view
seem sheer exuberant excess, does it not at once affirm the
beauty of life and stress the seasonless, fruitless nature of
all doings in the abyss? That pitchy river of the Barrators
will be busy enough with varied activities as the canto
develops, but it will serve to mend or to make nothing.

I would like to cite one more example of the contrast-
stressing image before quitting the *Inferno*. In Canto
XXXII, 31–35, we read of the Traitors to their Kin, frozen
in the ice of the lowest circle:

E come a gracidar si sta la rana
col muso fuor de l'acqua, quando sogna
di spigolar sovente la villana;

livide insin là dove appar vergogna
eran l'ombre dolenti nella ghiaccia,

. . . . .

And as the croaking bullfrog lies with muzzle above
water, in the season that makes the farm-girl dream
of harvesting;

livid up to the place where shame appears, the sor-
rowing shades were fixed in ice . . .

A strange comparison, with an effect that eludes analysis
—pleasing on first reading, puzzling when thought is focussed on it, and even ultimately displeasing to some readers, who offer the logical objection that the two sets of
terms contradict one another. The frog is, to be sure, a
happy creature surrounded by his favourite element, and
the peasant woman's dream is a good one—while the shivering souls are cramped in ice. But observe: once again
Dante has given a good deal of imagery in excess of the
actual comparison; the *stated likeness* pairs only the immersion of the frog with his muzzle above water and the
immersion of the sinners with their cheeks above the ice.
The farm girl, who seems to be introduced merely as a
feature of the season, and who remains totally outside the
stated comparison, is nonetheless very much inside and
part of the whole image and its working. She and the frog
together form a minute picture of tranquil summer
warmth with its promise of crops for gleaning in another
season. Drawn into the narrative by the slight link of the
immersion comparison, they perform the true poetic action of the passage, silently affirming that in the lake of
ice there are no comfortable creatures, no autumn, no
harvest and no dream of fair futures.

Purgatorio

The contrast-stressing image disappears from the poem
in the second canticle, where the things seen, puzzling
though they may be, are not life-parodies as they so often
were in Hell. Purgatory is the realm of recognition and
recovery—a step by step husking off of error and acquisition of true vision. The pilgrim's increasing understanding
is reflected in the comparisons which more and more

clearly and penetratingly point beyond what things *look* like, to what they *are* like. As in the *Inferno*, there are a number of minor similes and metaphors in which like sensuous terms are compared. There are sensuous comparisons with "expansive" overtones, of the kind discussed in the preceding section. There is a greatly increased number of simple metaphors based mainly on analogies of function and on personifications.[4] And there is, further, a small but startling group of extended comparisons with deeper and more complex interpretive insight than anything found in the earlier canticle.

> *Quando si parte il gioco de la zara*
> *colui che perde si riman dolente,*
> *repetendo le volte, e tristo impara:*

> *con l'altro se ne va tutta la gente;*
> *qual va dinanzi, e qual di dietro il prende,*
> *e qual da lato li si reca a mente:*

> *el non s'arresta, e questo e quello intende:*
> *a cui porge la man, più non fa pressa;*
> *e così dalla calca si difende.*

> *Tal era io in quella turba spessa,*
> *volgendo a loro, e qua e là, la faccia,*
> *e promettendo mi sciogliea da essa.*

When the game of dice breaks up, the one who loses stays behind, disconsolate, repeating the throws—and learns unhappily.

The others all surround the parting winner, one snatching at his coat-tails, one in front, another at his side, importunate.

He does not stop, and still he hears them all; those he holds out his hand to press no more, and this is his defence against the throng.

---

[4] As when Charles of Valois is said to have caused *Florence's paunch to burst*; when judgment *garners and winnows good and evil loves*; when the penitents of the fourth Terrace go *biting at sloth*; and so on.

Such was I in that crowded gathering; turning my
face to them, this way and that, and promising what
they asked, I freed myself.

VI, 1–12

Here once more the visual scene is very strong, but
manifestly it is not all the writer intends us to see. Super-
ficially the comparison tells us that the pilgrim now sees
himself to be like a winner in a dice game, moving on his
way through a press of importunate onlookers, granting
their requests (as his rare destiny allows), yet showing
something like impatience to resume his journey so that
he may enjoy his "prize". And the poet does not limit the
likeness to some specific aspect of the image—does not say
"so did I save myself from them" or "thus was I peti-
tioned", but simply "such was I". This invites us to accept
the comparison in all its terms. But can we? Is gaming
not somewhat out of the key of heavenward journeying?
And where in Purgatory is there anyone to match the disconsolate loser who opens the imaged scene? Though one
must puzzle over this loser, it is he who eventually furnishes the key to the whole passage. So firmly drawn in
the first three lines that one does not forget him when
the winner takes over, he eventually leads the reader to
his unmentioned and invisible counterpart in the pilgrim's
journey—someone *like the pilgrim*, a player of the same
game, therefore not one of the members of Purgatory at
all, but another wanderer of the Dark Wood, staking his
life on an unlikely chance—and one for whom no rescuing
Virgil came. And now we know what "game" they played
and why the word "game" is chosen. For the *odds stood
against* the pilgrim in the Dark Wood; it was *a toss-up*
whether he was to be saved or lost. His own will and action
had brought him to that pass (as the gamester to the
table), but neither was sufficient to ensure victory. Thus it
was not in reward of merit but by the mysterious opera-
tion of divine grace (the fall of the dice) that a rescuer
appeared, virtually assuring the living pilgrim of his even-
tual prize of rebirth. *That he might not have appeared,*

the image does not allow us to forget. The shadowy figure
of the loser reminds us of the terrible truth that not every
striver in the Dark Wood emerges from it happily. One
man is chosen, another left behind to "repeat the throws"
and "learn unhappily". And no honest winner of either
"game" can claim the winning number as a due reward.[5]

If the reader of this essay feels that I may be finding
more in the gaming image than is actually there, I would
beg him to read the passage again in context. Its meaning
emerges slowly: at the pace, one might say, with which
such ideas detach themselves from such experience. This
comparison, if I am not mistaken, is an instance of the
unexampled depth and density of Dante's art. In it he
sounds a note of pride in the haste and assurance of the
prizewinning pilgrim and a counternote of profound humility in the implied awareness of the loser's equal right.
Lines which at first seem a mere passing sharpener of pictorial clarity hold the clue to that synthesis of impersonal
life-pride with personal humility which the pilgrim is only
to achieve along with the final goal of his journey.

I will be brief with the metaphors of the *Purgatorio*,
citing only two typical examples—one relatively simple, the
other complex.[6] Visual clarity is no longer of moment in
them; they require interpretation, and they, in return, interpret the pilgrim's condition of quickened insight. With
the very different final metaphors of the *Paradiso* in mind,
I should like to stress the point that these are analytic in
nature; however instantaneously the mind may work to
grasp them, however deeply it may read them, it does so
by logical breakdown of subject and image. For this reason
analysis on the reader's part can, where at all called for,

[5] Dante is perfectly clear throughout the poem that grace rather
than any personal virtue has brought about the pilgrim's rescue
and elevation.

[6] Let the reader who doubts that true metaphors are numerous
in the *Purgatorio*, or that they are interpretive, examine some
single canto and take count. In the one with which we have just
been dealing (the sixth), for example, he will find metaphors in
37–38, 44–45, 76–79, 88–96, 112–114, 130–133, 142–144.

hope to do the greater rather than the lesser job of clari-
fication.

When Beatrice upbraids the pilgrim for his earlier wanderings from her (XXXI, 2–3) the harshness of her words
is expressed in

> volgendo suo parlare a me per punta
> che pur per taglio m'era paruto acro,

turning her discourse pointwise towards me, which
even edgewise had seemed sharp,

How speech can be a sword we can grasp only through
interpretation; the image says nothing intelligible to the
eye. Beatrice's speech, then, is piercingly sharp because it
reveals a truth now become grievous; thus it is no less
sharp when its touch is indirect (turned edgewise, as it
had been a moment earlier in Beatrice's account of the
pilgrim's "fall" to the pitying angels) than when pointed
towards the victim. The metaphor "adds to what we see"
a lesson in the role of love, and newly characterizes the
beauteous beloved. Beatrice is like Christ: she is an avenue
of love and, though supremely merciful, a merciless sword-
bearer.

Canto XIX, 61–67, gives a metaphor of a different
order, followed by a twin analogy. Virgil has just explained
to his bewildered pupil the nature of his siren dream,
with its danger and its attraction. He adds:

> "Bastiti, e batti a terra le calcagne:
> li occhi rivolgi al logoro che gira
> lo rege etterno con le rote magne."

> Quale il falcon, che prima d' piè si mira,
> indi si volge al grido e si protende
> per lo disio del pasto che là il tira;

> tal mi fec'io . . .

"Let this suffice. Now strike the earth with your heels
and fix your eyes again upon the lure which the eternal king spins with the great wheels."

Like falcon which looks down, first, at the ground,
then, turning towards the call, springs into flight,
hungering for the food that draws him there;

such I became . . .

One does not grasp the meaning of the first triplet until
one has read the second, which makes it clear that the
pilgrim is being likened to a falcon, urged to take flight
from his earthbound preoccupation and to follow the
"lure" of his true goal, the upper heavens. The man-falcon
metaphor of this first triplet is present by implication
only, in the series of commands. There is no visual likeness to support it. The pilgrim has been walking slowly
upward in the pass that leads from the penitents of Sloth
to those of Avarice; he is gazing at the ground, thinking
of the awful deception within his dream. It is just this
that Virgil wants to break through—this dream-bound
movement of a man who is awake and is on Mt Purgatory.
Impatient, Virgil tosses him a three-line explanation of
the dream (its content of false vision and corrective), and
then, with "let this suffice", scolds him into being a falcon.
But it is not flight alone which this bird image suggests—
not merely upward glance and motion such as Virgil
urges on the pilgrim. The poet has chosen the falcon rather
than any other bird because the trained falcon (an indis-
pensable accessory of the mediaeval hunt) has learned to
shape its instinctive behaviour to the service of a master,
hunting as another and greater hunter wills. All the terms
of the metaphor (61–63) unfold when the analogy
(64–66) throws this light back upon them. The pilgrim is
urged to take upward flight ("strike the earth with your
heels") like a homing falcon, in response to the will (the
"call") of the "king", who is God, who is the pilgrim's
falconer. The king calls him with the "lure" (in falconry
the word refers to a pair of simulated bird-wings used to
attract the hunting bird back to its starting point) of the
highest revolving heaven. Thus the passage repeats a
theme that runs throughout the poem: man's goal is at
the same time his point of departure (the soul's source)
which forever beckons him back. And it suggests that

God's will neither compels obedience (the falcon need not return to the hunter's wrist), nor does it require distortion of the creature's nature: the faculties man is asked to use are the best of those he was born with and the goal proposed one that offers "food" to his "hungering".

Paradiso

Again the nature of the place determines the language of comparison. Or seems to; for what place is it, really? No "place" at all—or, if you like, eight heavenly bodies, encased in concentric crystalline spheres, and two empty crystalline spheres, of which the outermost only is the proper abode of the blest.[7] As "place" the heavens are like so many movie-screens which serve as temporary projection centres for an essentially spaceless reality. In this they are unlike the circles of Inferno and the mountain of Purgatory which are there and are functional on the literal level.[8] Furthermore, the whole experience of Paradise, with the exception of the final (uncommunicable) vision, is itself a series of metaphorical appearances. This important fact is made clear by Beatrice (XXX, 76–81) where she invites the pilgrim to drink from the Empyrean river, the last of the many symbol-masks under which he has viewed reality, in order to dissolve that final disguise and see the real reality. Paradise is beyond space and time; its sights and events are merely educational concessions to the pilgrim's mortal condition, helping him to grasp by analogy what he cannot grasp directly: the nature of pure being, free from all becoming, from all contingency. Says Beatrice:

> Così parlar conviensi al vostro ingegno,
> però che solo da sensato apprende
> ciò che fa poscia d'intelletto degno.

[7] Cf. IV, 28–39

[8] Not an altogether accurate statement. It would perhaps be better to say that in the first eight heavens literal space begins a kind of withering away which is achieved in the ninth. See XXVII, 109–111.

Such speech suits the condition of your mind which
only from the senses learns what it then proffers to
the intellect.

IV, 40–42

In other words, because he is still incompletely "transhumanized", the pilgrim must be taught through the old
avenues of sense and the old mode of absolute individua-
tion. To see with the mind's eye and to see the universe
as one, is the ultimate goal. The pilgrim has come all the
way from the world of discrete, self-bounded things to the
edge of the heaven of unitary being—from fragmentation
and chaos to the doorstep of wholeness and harmony.

If the metaphor is truly a revealer of relationships,
bridging categories in order to point out likenesses hith-
erto unperceived, the showers of metaphors in the *Paradiso*
(like all proper members of the species) may be said to
play their part in the final goal—namely, the bringing together of the fragments of a whole which the world continually shatters. And, since the pilgrim in Paradise is no
longer restricted to seeing the accidental and impermanent
qualities of things, one would expect him to grasp, not
only likenesses within the concrete sensuous world, but
others bridging the distance between the concrete and the
abstract, between the real and the imaginary, and still
others between purely conceptual entities. All these we
find.

As one might foresee, concrete sensuous likeness plays a
diminished role in the *Paradiso*. (In the first ten cantos
there are not more than eight metaphors and comparisons
based truly on sensuous likeness.) Because the poet
ascribes no final reality to the space and time of this
realm, his imagery, like his narrative, must lead away from
the concrete reference and the analytic view toward the
suprasensual and the unitive. By the time we reach Canto
XVIII, where the souls of the Just are seen as lights forming the figure of an eagle and spelling out a Biblical motto
in sky-writing, appearances *qua* appearances are absurd.
We are not to stare at them; we are to take them as clues,

alone—clues to the nature of that which human minds cannot see without visual aids: the varieties of heavenly being. And so, when that eagle prepares to answer the pilgrim's questions and we read:

> *Quasi falcone ch'esce del cappello,*
> *move la testa e con l'ali si plaude,*
> *voglia mostrando e faccendosi bello,*

> *vid'io farsi quel segno, che di laude*
> *della divina grazia era contesto,*
> *con canti quai si sa chi là su gaude.*

Like falcon liberated from the hood, who shakes his head and claps his wings, showing his will and making himself beautiful,

so moved that standard woven all of praises, for grace divine, with songs such as are known to the rejoicing souls above . . .

XIX, 34-39

there is nothing (or worse) to be got from a sensuous comparison of the terms, either of the analogy (like falcon . . . so . . . that standard) or the metaphor that springs from it (standard woven of praises); whereas interpretation yields not only a deep insight into the joyousness of the response, but a glimpse of the perfect unity of these souls, who appear as one thing, respond as one, and are woven of one uniquely spiritual substance. Once again the peculiar relationship of the trained falcon—for whom the hunt is a requirement of his own nature—to the master in whose service he is sent forth ("liberated from the hood"), serves Dante to express the soul's relationship of free subjection to God.[9]

The falcon passage is typical of the major group of comparisons relating two concrete terms. Comparable to it are those to be found in I, 49-54; IV, 115-116; X, 139-148; among others. In all, the substance or the actions of Paradise are likened to earthly substances or actions so

[9] Cf. remarks on the falcon image of *Purg.* XIX, above.

that the pilgrim may make his approach to them; but it is an unfamiliar, unlifelike concrete that we see here, in a text that drives us constantly toward the comprehension of essences. The reader cannot rest in the concrete Paradise, for it contains no recognizable shapes or familiar behaviour. Nor does the poet want him to rest there.

There is a further extremely large group of comparisons and metaphors in which concrete *images* are paired with abstract *subjects*.[10] In the first two cantos, fifteen out of twenty-one metaphors seem to me to be of this variety, having such subjects as *motion, reason, wonder, desire, wisdom, order, being, providence*, etc. The effect of these is to reinforce the substantiality of ideas—an essential trait of Paradise. I quote three examples from this group:

> . . . *ciò procede*
> *da perfetto veder, che, come apprende*
> *così nel bene appreso move il piede.*

this comes of perfect vision which, as it apprehends, puts forth its foot into the apprehended good.

V, 4–6

> *O insensata cura de' mortali,*
> *quanto son difettivi sillogismi*
> *quei che ti fanno in basso batter l'ali!*

O foolish cares of mortals, how blundering those syllogisms are that make you downward beat your wings!

XI, 1–3

> *Però nella giustizia sempiterna*
> *la vista che riceve il vostro mondo,*
> *com'occhio per lo mare, entro s'interna.*

Such vision as is granted to your world in the eternal justice penetrates as does the eye into the ocean's depths.

XIX, 58–60

[10] In separating the two essential terms involved in metaphor, I designate as *subject* the term denoting what is to be characterized, and as *image* the term denoting that with which the *subject* term is identified.

And finally there is the somewhat smaller group of astonishing analogies where neither *subject* nor *image* is drawn from the concrete[11]:

> *Tu credi che a me tuo pensier mei*
> *da quel ch'è primo, così come raia*
> *dall'un, se si conosce, il cinque e 'l sei.*

You judge that your thought comes to me out of the primal mind, as from the one, if it be known, ray out the five and six.

XV, 55–57

> *. . . come veggion le terrene menti*
> *non capere in triangol due ottusi,*
>
> *così vedi le cose contingenti*
> *anzi che sieno in sè, mirando il punto*
> *a cui tutti li tempi son presenti;*

. . . as earthly minds perceive two obtuse angles will not fit the triangle,

so do you see contingent things before they come to be, fixing your gaze upon that point to which all times are present.

XVII, 14–18

So much for clear categories. But there are metaphors in the later cantos of the *Paradiso* which make nonsense of classification. For example, these words of the just souls —following their reminder that God, as the very ground of man's idea of justice, cannot himself be unjust, however much the brevity or obscurity of human sight may tempt man to suppose him so:

> *Lume non è, se non vien dal sereno*
> *che non si turba mai; anzi è tenebra,*
> *od ombra della carne, o suo veleno.*

[11] Both the immediately following quotations concern the nature of heavenly seeing; the first is spoken by the pilgrim's ancestor, Cacciaguida, to his descendant; the second by the pilgrim to Cacciaguida.

There is no light except from that serene which
never clouds; all else is darkness or shadow of the
flesh, or else its poison.

                                        XIX, 64–66

And these of the pilgrim when he looks round at Paradise after his professions of faith, hope and charity:

> *Ciò ch'io vedeva mi sembiava un riso*
> *dell'universo . . .*

That which I saw seemed to me a smile of the universe . . .

                                        XXVII, 4–5

And finally these of Beatrice concerning the last of the
symbol-masks under which the pilgrim must view the
heavenly host:

> *. . . Il fiume e li topazii*
> *ch'entrano ed escono ed il rider dell'erbe*
> *son di lor vero umbriferi prefazii.*

. . . The river and the topazes that plunge and rise,
and the laughter of the grasses are shadowy prefaces
of their reality.

                                        XXX, 76–78

These three royal metaphors, terse statements of essential moments in the progress towards heavenly wisdom, derive their *images* from flashes of intuitive clarity and imaginative synthesis so sharp and unified that logical analysis is quite beside the point. Such images, indeed, lightly
and happily contradict the logic of intellect in a way
Dante, I think, would never have tolerated in the first two
canticles, which are reason's realm.

It is not that one cannot make rational sense of these
passages if one cares to try. But at best such an attempt
can merely show us how better to focus our thought on
the original words, which embody a synthesis incapable
of paraphrase, a perception grotesquely altered by any

change.[12] The first of these passages, if we read it in
context, affirms that all seeming "light" other than that of
God, is a false semblance; it names three varieties of such
non-light: darkness, shadow of the flesh and "poison" of the
flesh. Darkness *which is taken as light* may well be the
condition of the intellect without aid of faith; shadow of
the flesh may be the obscurity cast by pride, greed and lust
across what otherwise might have been viewed in true
light; and "poison", the more deadly emanation of the
actual deeds of pride, greed and lust. But Dante does not
ask us to think about what these terms denote; we have
passed through the realms of darkness and flesh-shadow
in his poem, and now need merely allow these terms to
expand in the mind. To the best of our individual capaci-
ties to understand them, we will do so through the images
and associations they call up. In other words, nothing is
to be gained here, no further penetration achieved, by
analysis.

Nothing like this is to be found in the *Inferno* or in the
Purgatorio, where a certain exactitude of reference is the
norm and where generally both terms (subject and object)
of metaphors are drawn from realms of man's daily experience—one being used literally, the other figuratively.
Here one might say that both terms are figurative; for the
false light or lightlessness implied in the subject (the "it"
which is "no light") is no more a physical illumination than
the "darkness" of the *image*. Or one might perhaps venture
the very opposite, upon suspicion that in this equation of
two "figurative" entities we have actually passed beyond
metaphor and emerged on its far side in a new simple
equivalence, within a world where all light is spiritual.

I will not labour this last; but were Dante's intention
of that kind, it would be merely one further matching of
the pilgrim's vision to the high goal of the journey which,
above all, has educated his eyes. In the illusory solid In-

[12] And, in the Italian original, associations and musical qualities
of surpassing importance, which no translation could hope to ap-
proximate.

fernal world he "saw the scene"—no more; in Purgatory he saw meaning within the ordered scene and in the visions of the imagination; in Paradise his glance has passed beyond the scene altogether, has passed the symbolic as well as the literal masks, and finally has come to rest, simply and immediately, upon essential being.

(b) A CODA TO METAPHOR AND COMPARISON

The whole bent of Dante's imagination is so strongly towards the casting of ideas in the form of images, that to hang a sampling of his metaphors high and dry, as I have done in the preceding pages, is to give no idea either of the great variety and quantity of the minor imagery generally, or of the way in which minor images are related to the bigger imaginative and speculative movements of the poem. Actually, the texture of the work as it strikes the reader on any given page is qualified above all by the rapid and energetic succession of sharp sensuous impressions, supported by metaphors and comparisons, and by their almost musical relationship to the developing themes.

What follows is a close examination of a brief typical passage of Dante's book, with the object of discovering some of the details of such texture, and some of the qualities that make almost every page of the *Comedy* at once lucid, bold in outline, and subtly dense in imaginative experience. I will not insist that my passage is perfectly representative, since I think it is doubtful that any fifty lines taken from any of the three canticles could be representative of the whole work with its changing dramatic emphasis and its gradual expansion of philosophic thought. I have looked merely for a brief transitional passage without dramatic or symbolic high points; and have selected the opening section of *Inferno* XXXII, more or less at random among a number that came to hand suiting my conditions.

1   S'io avessi le rime aspre e chiocce,
       come si converrebbe al tristo buco
       sovra 'l qual pontan tutte l'altre rocce,

     io premerei di mio concetto il suco
       più pienamente; ma perch'io non l'abbo,
       non sanza tema a dicer mi conduco;

     chè non è impresa da pigliare a gabbo
       discriver fondo a tutto l'universo,
       nè da lingua che chiami mamma o babbo:

     ma quelle donne aiutino il mio verso
       ch'aiutaro Anfione a chiuder Tebe,
       sì che dal fatto il dir non sia diverso.

     Oh sovra tutte mal creata plebe
       che stai nel luogo onde parlare è duro,
       mei foste state qui pecore o zebe!

     Come noi fummo giù nel pozzo scuro
       sotto i piè del gigante assai più bassi,
       e io mirava ancora all'alto muro,

     dicere udi'mi: "Guarda come passi;
       va sì, che tu non calchi con le piante
       le teste de' fratei miseri lassi."

     Per ch'io mi volsi, e vidimi davante
       e sotto i piedi un lago che per gelo
       avea di vetro e non d'acqua sembiante.

     Non fece al corso suo sì grosso velo
       di verno la Danoia in Osterlicchi,
       nè Tanaì là sotto il freddo cielo,

     com'era quivi; che se Tambernicchi
       vi fosse su caduto, o Pietrapana,
       non avrìa pur dall'orlo fatto cricchi.

     E come a gracidar si sta la rana
       col muso fuor dell'acqua, quando sogna
       di spigolar sovente la villana;

34 *livide, insin là dove appar vergogna*
    eran l'ombre dolenti nella ghiaccia,
    mettendo i denti in nota di cicogna.

    Ognuno in giù tenea volta la faccia:
    da bocca il freddo, e dalli occhi il cor tristo
    tra lor testimonianza si procaccia.

    Quand'io m'ebbi dintorno alquanto visto,
    volsimi a' piedi, e vidi due sì stretti,
    ch 'l pel del capo avìeno insieme misto.

    "Ditemi, voi che si strignete i petti,"
    diss'io, "chi siete?" E quei piegaro i colli;
    e poi ch'ebber li visi a me eretti,

    li occhi lor, ch'eran pria pur dentro molli,
    gocciar su per le labbra, e 'l gelo strinse
    le lacrime tra essi e riserrolli.

    Con legno legno spranga mai non cinse
    forte così; ond'ei come due becchi
51 *cozzaro insieme, tanta ira li vinse.*

If I had rhymes rough and hoarse, as would befit the dismal hole, on which all the other rocky steeps converge and weigh,

I should press out the juice of my conception more fully; but since I have them not, not without fear I bring myself to tell thereof:

for to describe the bottom of all the universe is not an enterprise for being taken up in sport, nor for a tongue that cries mamma and papa.

But may those ladies help my verse who helped Amphion with walls to close in Thebes; so that my words may not be diverse from the fact.

O ye beyond all others, miscreated rabble, who are in the place, to speak of which is hard, better had ye here on earth been sheep or goats!

When we were down in the dark pit, under the Giant's feet, much lower, and I still was gazing at the high wall,

I heard a voice say to me: "Look how thou passest: take care with thy soles thou tread not on the heads of the weary wretched brothers."

Whereat I turned myself, and saw before me and beneath my feet a lake, which through frost had the semblance of glass and not of water.

Never did the Danube of Austria make so thick a veil for his course in winter, nor the Don afar beneath the frigid sky,

as there was here: for if Tambernic had fallen on it, or Pietrapana, it would not even at the edge have given a creak.

And as the frog to croak sits with his muzzle out of the water, when the peasant-woman oft dreams that she is gleaning:

so, livid, up to where the hue of shame appears, the doleful shades were in the ice, sounding with their teeth like storks.

Each held his face turned downwards; by the mouth their cold, and by the eyes the sorrow of their hearts is testified amongst them.

When I had looked round a while I turned towards my feet; and saw two so pressed against each other that they had the hair of their heads intermixed.

"Tell me, ye who thus together press your bosoms," said I, "who you are." And they bended their necks; and when they had raised their faces towards me,

their eyes, which only inwardly were moist before, gushed at the lids, and the frost bound fast the tears between them and closed them up again.

Wood with wood no cramp did ever gird so strongly;
wherefore they, like two he-goats, butted one another;
such rage came over them.

XXXII, 1–51

One can immediately observe in this passage the crossing and interweaving of the two main directional lines
along which the poet's imagination constantly works: the
one projecting the world of the journey—in this case the
last circle of Hell—the other radiating outward and backward into the living world: into myth, history, art and
personal vicissitude. The first projects what the traveller's
eye sees; the second, the responses of memory and imagination, exploring and qualifying.

These two related lines in their fundamental relationship to the form of the work, characterize the texture of
the poem as much as any quality it possesses. They under-
lie and integrate the enormous variety of the minor imagery. They make the beauty of metaphor and allusion the
fulfilment of an inner necessity. For the external form
of the poem is a journey, while its theme is the education
and salvation of a living man (one must not forget for an
instant that this poem ends in a return to life), and thus
naturally and necessarily its reference is always twofold,
moving from the visionary world that reduces life to its
essences, back to the solid world with its hieroglyphic
masks.

Both lines start in the poet's here and now of writing,
after the completion of the journey in which he was the
principal actor, and from an unidentified desk somewhere
in Italy. And this matters in the experience of the reader,
since the narrator's "I" refers actually to two distinct perspectives. The first of these "I's"—the one with which our
present passage begins—is, with respect to the journey,
safely and fully possessed of its facts and its meanings,
and has merely its realization in poetry to wrestle with;
the other is in process of making, suffering and seeking to
understand the journey, and thus is different at every successive point of the narration. The reader, given both

perspectives, must distinguish and unify the twofold variable view. (It is in order to keep the two distinct that I have called one speaker *Dante* and the other *the pilgrim,* throughout these chapters.) If the reader fails to keep them apart, he will miss something of Dante's intention. The *Comedy* is, as it were, played as drama on one level of a stage, while from another the narrating poet sometimes halts the action to comment on it.

Lines 1–17 of our present passage is a set of reflections of this latter kind. It thus asks us to take its judgments as final in the author's view; which is quite otherwise from the way in which we must take the pilgrim's judgments and emotions on the actual stage of Hell. Accordingly, his remarks on that art by which the world is to be more or less accurately apprised of his vision of Hell are to be taken as mature and serious views. For Dante is not merely complaining here about the difficulty of writing the *Comedy*; nor urging us to pay terrified attention to what is coming in his story. He is saying something which he means both seriously and relevantly about the nature of art: namely, that the conception of the artist can never be rendered perfectly in the finished work, because his medium is not flawlessly transparent. Cast in the form of a rather dubious metaphor, the idea is apt at first to be rather quickly passed over. The poet's conception, we are told, is a sort of fruit from which he cannot fully press out the juice, since he does not possess words "rough and hoarse" enough ("aspre e chiocce" instantly suggest to ear and imagination the qualities he wants) to match the lowest depth of Hell. A second image—"tongue that cries mamma and papa"—intensifies the first, saying that in the face of his present subject he is no better equipped than a lisping infant: the sort of words he needs do not exist.

Interesting though this is—the first broaching of the problem of idea in its relation to material form—its full weight is not to be detected until a certain stir of reverberations is set up from it by a very different approach in a later part of the poem. We have seen this happen elsewhere; it is a trait of Dante's composing to state a theme in one part of the poem and then, without notice, to resume it under a different light (or to exhibit another facet of it) under quite different circumstances, later on. Actually, by the time we have reached Canto XXXII of *Inferno* we have already heard hints that poem-making is comparable to world-making. As we go on, we see every feature of the one treated in language that brings out its analogy to the other. Thus our present passage will be called to mind again by *Paradiso* XIII, 52–79, which, in discussing the relation of the divine conception to *its* material vehicle, seeks to suggest also the poet's problem in all its main terms: the divine light flooding the creative mind; the projection of that light into a material mould, and the resulting discrepancy between the idea and its rendering.

Dante does not make this audacious comparison explicit. But its force is unlikely to escape the reader who has been following in the poem its author's constant concern with the objectification of the poetic conception. This is especially clear when we look ahead from the passage we have been studying, to *Paradiso* XIII. Each passage recalls and reinforces the other, and both imply a Platonic injunction to try to penetrate the substantial shapes of all things in search of their ideal essences. In *Inferno* XXXII the poet says, in effect, that according to the measure of eloquence his poem here needs, it lisps in infant syllables. He calls on the Muses to help him—as they helped Amphion, the wall-builder of Thebes, by causing the stones to leap into their places. The myth, entering here, is like a little breeze from another direction. But it is not introduced idly. It reminds us of what the guardian geniuses of creativity can do: they can infuse life into brute substance. It suggests that a similar power might send the recalcitrant words springing forward to say what Dante saw in his imagination.

In line 13, without pause, the poet addresses the rabble of Hell directly and scornfully. There is no hiatus between this and what precedes, since this rabble *is* the conception for which he lacks fitting words. These souls are his prob-

lem, and he is their second doom, for his poem intends
to give them a second life. Better indeed had they "on
earth been sheep or goats": they have created Hell, and
must bear both its brunt and that of the poem which
means to put them forever in the world's eye.[13]

With line 16 the reader's flexible perspective is shifted
back to the pilgrim and his immediate situation in the
lowest circle of Hell. The journey has come close to the
end of its first stage; we are down in the "dark pit", below
the feet of the giants, below everything, in the "bottom
of the universe", the "dismal hole on which all other rocky
steeps converge and weigh"—thus by implication with the
full pressure of the world's weight of evil upon us. There
is no light here other than the false light of treacherous
intellect, and under it the glare of the ice that forms naturally where all love is cut off. Every detail of the general
image stands in strict opposition to what we are to see
much later, at the loftiest point of the voyage: here we
have darkness instead of absolute light, cold hatred instead of absolute love, an icy lake instead of an unfolding
celestial flower, souls rigidly bound and underfoot instead
of souls freely and loftily assembled, the congealed tears
of the abyss instead of the "smile of the universe".

The second "I", which emerges here—the "I" of memory—can tell us what he saw and heard, but not what the
scene meant, since he understood too little of it; nor even
what he felt, since he was not conscious of the icy damage
this lowest pit of Hell had done to his human emotions.
In such a situation Dante's graphic genius is wonderfully
inventive. He can say everything he wants to say, to the
eye alone. He shows us persons, places, actions peeled
clean of his own interpretations and of subjective qualifi-
cations. And he shows us sensations and emotions, by
implications carried in the visible scene and action. Thus,
for example, the stance of the pilgrim at the beginning of
the episode, with his gaze fixed on the wall from which he
has just been handed down, and not the slightest awareness of the lake of ice beneath his feet, suggests a spastic

13 Cf. *Par.* XVII, 112–142

terror. The structure of the sentence that tells us about this, is in itself extremely interesting: its main clause, "I heard a voice say to me", which is to introduce the crucial news that the dead lie underfoot, is virtually muffled by the two dependent clauses that precede it and block it with their burden of information. There is consequently a certain flatness and quietness about the main clause when it does enter that belies the extraordinariness of what is to come. Again, in the utterance of the voice from underfoot there is a delaying of the real core of interest by the two imperatives: "Look how thou passest: take care. . . ." Finally, after all this, the astonishing news that the dead are somewhere here glued in the ice and imperilled by careless feet reaches us by a mere implication rather than a direct statement. The result is that the reader must rivet his attention on these words if he is to follow their drift; and so is made to feel through one more channel the resistance to comprehension, the choked obscurity of the place.

The pilgrim at length brings his eyes down from the wall and looks about him and sees that he is standing at the edge of a lake of ice. There follows in the next eighteen lines a general description of the place. These are eighteen lines of intensely energetic experience for the eye, which is first brought to bear on the glassy substance underfoot, then projected back to earth to consider the rivers Don and Danube in winter; thence to the mountains, Tambernic and Pietrapana in Italy[14]; next centred on a close view of a scene from simple rural life, and finally returned to Hell to see the souls fastened in the ice-lake, their physical attitudes and the appearance of their misery.

In this whole intensely graphic series the eye is put to work in the service of feeling. Ostensibly the two opening comparisons ("never did the Danube . . . ; nor the Don . . .") and the allusions that follow are intended to convey some idea of the thickness of Cocytus' ice. On this

[14] The whereabouts of Tambernic is, actually, uncertain. Commentators disagree on what mountain Dante was referring to.

basis they might be called quaintly redundant. Effectively, however, they do another sort of work: they remind us that the living world is there, above, while we are here in Hell, and they create a sense of grave distances, deep silence and intense, immeasurable foreign cold. Under the "thick veil" of the Danube's ice runs the diminished and invisible stream of its life. Over the Don rises a frigid sky. What these descriptions make us feel is carried over into our feelings about Cocytus, together with a heightened sense of imprisonment and ominousness. Tambernic and Pietrapana, earthly mountains, reinforce the sense of distances; but the bare hint of a demonism that could uproot them and bring them crashing on the infernal lake leaves a still stronger impression in imagination. Thus two absent rivers, two absent mountains and an event which is not scheduled to take place qualify the coldness, the silence and the remoteness of the pit.

The second analogy ("And as the frog to croak . . ."), linked to the mountain passage by its "and", shifts the visual perspective slightly, but plays a total change on the emotional one. Its sudden warmth and human tenderness come up sharply in contrast to the frozen images before and after it. Its correct logic (comparing the depth of the frog's immersion to the sinners') is, as was the logical statement about the rivers, a mere mask for its real impact: the nostalgia it suggests for the simple flow of natural life.[15]

The narrative, interrupted and delayed by the two analogies, and the speculation about falling mountains, resumes with line 34. Six lines give us the pilgrim's general glance at the damned in this outer ring of Cocytus—livid bodies fixed up to the neck in ice, retaining only so much human warmth as allows their teeth still to chatter and their eyes to weep. Both diction and syntax are eloquent here. The livid bodies are said to be buried "up to where the hue of shame appears"—a curious phrase over which we halt for a moment to discover that what it means is, simply, up to the throat. This circumlocution from Dante,

15 See above, pages 150–51, where this analogy is further studied.

who generally writes with a compression that takes one's
breath away, surprises. But actually it is neither accidental
nor unique; Dante not infrequently, when it suits his purpose, expands the statement of a denotation that might
have been put into a single word.[16] And here the purpose
of taking the long way round to say "throat" is to make us
see more than is actually there to be seen—indeed, the
sort of thing which it is impossible to see except as poetry
puts it before us: the *absence* of a "hue of shame" on
those throats and cheeks which ought to blush, but cannot, since they have lost the very capacity for shame.

The triplet 37–39 ("Each held his face turned downward . . .") shows a cunning of syntax. The grammatical
subjects and the verb of the second and third clauses—
their cold, the sorrow of their hearts, and *is testified*—involved no visual experience at all. But the placing of the
adverbial phrases, *by the mouth* and *by the eyes,* before
the grammatical subjects, and in stressed rhythmic posi-
tions, gives these effective dominance. In reading the
whole triplet one experiences the three descriptions as
though they were parallel, seeing first the downturned
heads, then the mouths with chattering teeth, then the
eyes weeping. The subjective experiences of the "cold"
and the "sorrow" thus do seem to reach us in visual terms.
Not the least striking effect of this rendering is its strict
impersonality—the utter detachment, even to the legalistic
language, of the observer who records it, and who has
evidently himself come a long way into the frost since we
saw him weep at the mere sound of the first wailing heard
in Hell.

Now this observer proceeds to look about him "a while",
and then to glance down at what lies closest to him. There
is real violence in this sudden drawing of the reader's eye
from the broad general view to the sharp close-up of "two
so pressed together that they had the hair of their heads
intermixed". The travesty of love in this embrace (of
brothers who in life were each other's murderers) is picked
out again in the pilgrim's address to them as "ye who to-

[16] Cf., for example, *Purg.* I, 49–51 and *Par.* XIII, 37–42

gether press your bosoms". The stress is still graphic; indeed, the poet will not release the reader's eye for a moment, but trusts his meaning to filter through things seen, in *felt* form.

Lines 44–48, beginning "And they bended their necks; and when they had raised their faces towards me . . .", is an example of Dante's strictly calculated economy. His pilgrim notes coldly, as is appropriate to his situation, exactly what his eyes take in, and nothing more. If the bending of the brother's necks is necessarily made painful by their locked position and the ice that comes to their throats, he does not feel it, and the poet does not record it. He makes the pathos of the tears that suddenly flood the brothers' eyes when their gaze reaches the free, living shape standing above them, more terrible by his imperviousness: he sets down with the utmost bareness the fact of the sudden weeping and its quick icing over. With cold precision he finds a simile to express the strength of the seal formed by the frozen tears. Then, immediately, he gives us another comparison that makes graphic the animal rage that blots out the single moment of human memory and regret. The two damned souls butt one another like goats. All that has been implied but not articulated in the brief passage adds to the intense impact of this ending: we know we are at the lowest pitch of Hell, where treachery has so frozen up the soul that the recollection of its lost humanity can scarcely break through; when by rare chance it does, the solvent of human tears becomes, ironically, the instrument of worse anguish. The two souls have not answered the pilgrim's question: they have merely looked up and been blinded back into their inhumanity. The last we see of them is their pair of goatlike butting heads. Heads that hatched their first fatal quarrel, and which are now trying to kill each other a second time.

The fifty-line passage ends here.

(c) THE IMAGE OF THE WORLD RECALLED

Era già l'ora che volge il disio
ai navicanti e 'ntenerisce il core
lo dì c'han detto ai dolci amici addio;

e che lo novo peregrin d'amore
punge, s'e' ode squilla di lontano
che paia il giorno pianger che si more.

'Twas now the hour that turns back the desire of those who sail the seas and melts their heart, that day when they have said to their sweet friends adieu,

and that pierces the new pilgrim with love, if from afar he hears the chimes which seem to mourn for the dying day.

Purg. VIII, 1–6

Come a man destra per salire al monte
dove siede la chiesa che soggioga
la ben guidata sopra Rubaconte,

si rompe del montar l'ardita foga
per le scalee che si fero ad etade
ch'era sicuro il quaderno e la doga;

così s'allenta la ripa che cade
quivi ben ratta dall'altro girone.

As on the right hand, to ascend the mount where stands the church which, over Rubaconte, dominates the well-guided city,

the bold scarp of the ascent is broken by the steps which were made in the times when the records and the measure were safe;

even so is the bank made easier, which here right steeply falls from the other cornice.

Purg. XII, 100–107

What Dante has done in these two images he does again and again, with many variations, throughout the three canticles: on the stages of Hell, Purgatory, Heaven he recalls the world—sometimes by direct allusion, often through analogy and comparison, now very briefly, now at length, sometimes tenderly, more often with great bitterness. Birds, beasts, cities, citizens, peasants, the days' labours on land and offshore, rivers, mountains, sunrises, dusk, snow and rain, over countries far from and close to Italy, and above all in Italy—a whole mosaic of glimpses of the "threshing-floor that makes us wax so fierce", scattered piecemeal through the otherworld.

It is of course not the *fact* of reference to the things of the world which impresses—since obviously it is to the world that both poet and souls must turn for reference if they are to compare or recollect at all. What I speak of is rather the cumulative effect of a continuous weaving through the poem of whole streams of allusions that reassemble the world from a point outside it, and qualify it, deeply and intensely colouring the whole poem. They form a running counterpoint to the abstracts of the human soul on which the poem centres.

One chain of such allusions links the members of the otherworld to the regions, towns, landscapes in which they were born or lived their lives:

> *Siede la terra dove nata fui*
> *su la marina dove 'l Po discende*
> *per aver pace co' seguaci sui.*

The town where I was born sits on the shore where Po descends to rest with his attendant streams.

Inf. V, 97–99

> *Io fui latino e nato d'un gran tosco:*
> *Guiglielmo Aldobrandesco fu mio padre.*

I was Italian and son of a great Tuscan: Guglielmo Aldobrandesco was my father.

Purg. XI, 58–59

Io fui abate in San Zeno a Verona
sotto lo 'mperio del buon Barbarossa,
di cui dolente ancor Melan ragiona.

I was Abbot of San Zeno at Verona, under the rule of the good Barbarossa, of whom Milan yet discourses with sorrow.

Purg. XVIII, 118–120

scias quod ego fui successor Petri.

Intra Sïestri e Chiaveri s'adima
una fiumana bella, e del suo nome
lo titol del mio sangue fa sua cima.

scias quod ego fui successor Petri.

Between Sestri and Chiaveri flows down a fair river, and from its name the title of my race takes origin.

Purg. XIX, 99–102

Intra Tupino e l'acqua che discende
del colle eletto dal beato Ubaldo,
fertile costa d'alto monte pende,

onde Perugia sente freddo e caldo
da Porta Sole; e di retro le piange
per grave giogo Nocera con Gualdo.

Between Tupino and the stream that drops from the hill chosen by the blessed Ubaldo, a fertile slope hangs from a lofty mount,

wherefrom Perugia feeleth cold and heat through Porta Sole, and behind it waileth Nocera, for the heavy yoke, and Gualdo.

Par. XI, 43–48

In all these both the form and the impulse that begets them is much the same. In the *Inferno* seven persons introduce themselves in this fashion; in the *Purgatorio* twelve do so; in the *Paradiso* six, while two others are similarly introduced by another speaker. Thus these pas-

sages, each of which is engaging in itself, form a connected
motif of their own in which the power of the individual
example is multiplied. They affirm the reality of place, of
an earthly site; and the importance to man of those spatial
and temporal reference points by which he knows his own
life as part of the life of his race. Indeed, most of Dante's
characters remember their lives not merely in terms of
personal circumstances but as having belonged to a particular "clan", place, social context and tradition. Some
of the diversity of Italian culture in the long stretch of
years upon which Dante drew is hinted here in the family
names, the royal courts, the monastic communities, the
cities, the factions and the guilds. But place dominates. It
stands first in virtually every one of the introductions to
which I have just referred. It is never omitted from them,
no matter what else may be; often it is exquisitely elaborated. For the cities that men have built and then marred,
it shows a rough angry love; for the mountains, valleys,
rivers and fields of Italy a deep lyric tenderness.

There is a second pattern of world-recall, related to this
first yet distinct from it, that heaps invective on the greedy
cities, and even on whole regions, of Italy, culminating in
an attack on the embroiled country at large. I count in
the *Comedy* sixteen such diatribes, great and small: one
addressed to Italy, two against the Romagna, one apiece
against Lombardy, Pisa, Genoa, Pistoia, the March of
Treviso—and fully eight against Florence. Rage, bitterness,
irony and an urgent call to order are in these. Some are
spoken in the voice of the poet, others by figures in the
fictional narrative, but all have the same tone of outrage:
these degenerated political communities are all candidates
for damnation. Florence, Dante's own dearly beloved and
hated native city, once the seat of all honour and virtue, is
now the prime example of vice. Her pride, greed, vanity
and mixture of stocks are all excoriated with bitter irony
or straight indignation. Hell is full of her citizens—both
Guelphs and Ghibellines. She is, in one stroke of irony,
"the well-guided one"; in another "thou rich, thou at peace,
thou so wise . . . who dost make such subtle provision,

that to mid-November reaches not what thou in October
spinnest"; and she is invited to rejoice in her greatness,
since "over land and sea thou beatest thy wings, and thy
name through Hell expands itself!" In bitterness she is
"our depraved city", refuge of "that ungrateful, malignant
people", coiner of "that accursed flower[17] which hath set
sheep and lambs astray". And so on, against the opposing
music of the beauties he remembers and his desire to return in peace to that "fair sheepfold".

Thus Dante's anger makes a pattern of recollection fas-
tening chiefly on the communities of men. And if we add
to it the still angrier invectives against the moral degenera-
tion of great families, of the monastic orders, of the priest-
hood up to its very summit, the accumulation makes a trail
of fire through the poem, flaming with greatest fierceness
close to God, and in the mouth of a saint. I refer to the
magnificent boldness of St Peter's:

> "Quelli ch'usurpa in terra il luogo mio,
>   il luogo mio, il luogo mio, che vaca
>   nella presenza del Figliuol di Dio,
>
> fatt'ha del cimiterio mio cloaca
>   del sangue e della puzza; onde 'l perverso
>   che cadde di qua su, là giù si placa."

"He who usurpeth upon earth my place, my place, my
place, which in the presence of the Son of God is
vacant,

hath made my burial-ground a conduit for that blood
and filth, whereby the apostate one who fell from
here above, is soothed down there below."

Par. XXVII, 22-27

A third stream of world-recalling passages is of a totally
different sort. It is composed of analogies that reach not
only back to earth but outside the explicit thematic scope
of the poem, bringing into it indirectly some of the innocent and unconscious aspects of life that have no place,

---

[17] The lily-stamped Florentine florin.

except by contrast, in the rigorous central substance. The motion of a reptile-shaped thief in Hell recalls the lizard which "beneath the mighty scourge of the canicular days, going from hedge to hedge, appears a flash of lightning, if it cross the way". The entrance to an upward passageway on Purgatory is so narrow that "A bigger opening many times the peasant hedges up with a little forkful of his thorns, when the grape is darkening". The penitent gluttons with their hands uplifted towards the leaves of the forbidden tree are "like spoilt and greedy children who beg, and he of whom they beg answers not, but to make their longing full keen, holds what they desire on high, and hides it not". Souls which appear as lights moving in a circle round the pilgrim in the Sun "seemed as ladies, not from the dance released, but pausing, silent, listening till they catch the notes renewed". And a mistaken interpretation of a momentary dark look on Virgil's face is the slender, but brilliantly welcome excuse for recalling how:

> *In quella parte del giovanetto anno*
> *che 'l sole i crin sotto l'Aquario tempra*
> *e già le notti al mezzo dì sen vanno,*
>
> *quando la brina in su la terra assempra*
> *l'imagine di sua sorella bianca,*
> *ma poco dura alla sua penna tempra;*
>
> *lo villanello a cui la roba manca,*
> *si leva, e guarda, e vede la campagna*
> *biancheggiar tutta; ond'ei si batte l'anca,*
>
> *ritorna in casa, e qua e là si lagna,*
> *come 'l tapin che non sa che si faccia;*
> *poi riede, e la speranza ringavagna,*
>
> *veggendo il mondo aver cangiata faccia;*
> *in poco d'ora, e prende suo vincastro,*
> *e fuor le pecorelle a pascer caccia.*

In that part of the youthful year, when the Sun tempers his locks beneath Aquarius, and the nights already wane towards half the day,

when the hoar-frost copies his white sister's image
on the ground, but short while lasts the temper of
his pen;

the peasant, whose fodder fails, rises and looks, and
sees the fields all white; whereat he smites his thigh,

goes back into the house and to and fro laments like
a poor wight who knows not what to do; then comes
out again and recovers hope,

observing how the world has changed its face in little
time; and takes his staff, and chases forth his lambs to
feed.

Inf. XXIV, 1–15

It is by the thread of such analogies that so many birds
and beasts are attached to the divine poem, each seized by
some quick exact stroke that sharpens them into life along
the margin of our attention. A continuous garland of these
creatures and simple scenes clings round the drama of the
otherworld, not unlike the flora and fauna carved on the
portals and columns of the mediaeval cathedral. In the
same garland we see children waking from sleep, grasping
their mothers' breasts, begging for trifles; and musicians
playing, ladies dancing, shipwrights building, cooks at
their pots, and peasants tilling. Briefest sketches, detached
from the narrative, present ostensibly as merest illustrations of some essentially different matter, these passages
have so firm a peripheral existence of their own that they
pass quite beyond the function for which they seem designed; they colour the whole context in which they occur,
and remain independently in memory. Of course, the more
attractive they are, individually, the more distracting their
presence ought to be, since the business of images is to
work within and for the text, and not to stand irrelevantly
on their own identity. But it is in fact from their work in
the text that these illustrations of Dante's get a large part
of their independent charm. All of them, whatever their
overt function, have, when they occur, the poignancy of
distant reminders; they suggest both living things and a

quality of livingness which is altogether remote from the otherworld mode. But the poignancy of this relationship clings to these images as well as to their subjects, and it remains with them even when one recalls them out of context. "As the cranes go chanting their lays . . ." is as marked by having been uttered in the first Circle of Hell as *Inferno* V is marked by its utterance. One is accordingly the more grateful to such lines for the life they assert. They are—all these images are—a series of life-lines tossed to the reader immersed in the otherworld. They bring him momentarily back to the surface of the innocent little globe which he has made so fierce; they put him in touch with its points of no moral stress or strain or stain. Thus they are bound into the poem and stamped by it, however one may take them out to hold up to the light. Further, having more in common than structure and earthly reference, they do not stand apart from one another but form a chain of similar reminders, having the same sort of energy and effect: a frieze of works and days that, for all its dependency puts its offerings of simplicity, order and comeliness into the experience of the great central ceremony of the poem.

Chapter VI

THE LADDER OF VISION

This much let me say however: God invented and gave us sight to the end that we might behold the courses of intelligence in the heaven, and apply them to the courses of our own intelligence which are akin to them, the unperturbed to the perturbed; and that we, learning them and partaking of the natural truth of reason, might imitate the absolutely unerring courses of God and regulate our own vagaries.

PLATO

There are certain symbolic images in Dante's poem—terms of its landscape or action—which lie in its foundation solidly and simply, yet with such profound suggestive power that even on a first reading one does not escape some feeling of their significance. The sun is such a symbol, and the human eye a related one; the journey, the abyss, the mountain are others. All these lead from the literal and concrete demonstrations of the poem to the subtlest regions of Dante's thought.

The moment we approach the first of these symbols— the sun, which takes precedence over all the others, both as an actual presence and as a figuration of divine and intellectual light—the whole poem comes down upon us in examples, flashing with related stars, flames, torches, sparks; and darkening with related caverns, thickets, clouds of smoke. And we note that however pressing the symbolic import of the light may grow to be, it continues to be rooted in vivid substantial portrayal: of unnatural and terrible dark-light in the *Inferno,* where "the sun is silent"; of natural light in the *Purgatorio,* where every hue and angle of the sun, from dawn to setting, is recorded with precision and delight; and of supernatural splendours in the third canticle where the primary source of all light, intellectual and physical, plays directly over the heavenly spheres, and the earthly sun is shown us under a revised perspective, as one of many vehicles of God.

These images are not mere embellishments in Dante. If physical light is the dominant image of the *Comedy,* that is because it is the natural link between the two extreme terms of the symbolic journey: man in the darkness and ignorance of error, desiring vision, and God whose being is absolute light. Nor is the symbolism which attaches to these images conventional, although it stems from a rich and familiar tradition. But precisely because the traditional symbols are present, the reader must be careful not to pass them by lightly under the supposition that he has heard all this before. He has not. Dante's thought is not contained in the received ideas from which he takes his start nor in the figurative elements he borrows. He moves beyond and around them in the far wider range to which his imagination and his medium have access.

Let us suppose, for instance, that the Old Testament is his earliest source for the simple, reverent equation of God with sun as power and light. In the typical Scriptural utterances—such as *The Lord God is a sun and a shield*[1] and *Come, let us walk in the light of the Lord*[2] there is a completed metaphorical assumption, bold and thrilling. But Dante does not adopt that assumption: rather, he gives us the experience that generated it—rediscovering it, and compelling the reader to rediscover it through the sheer blandishments of the physical light in Purgatory, after the escape from darkness. As though no word had ever been spoken on the subject before—or no word except that of the Greek myth-makers, from whom he borrowed attitudes

[1] Psalm lxxxiv   [2] Isaiah ii

and epithets to adorn the path to God—the poet devises
God in the animating presence of the natural sunlight on
the heaven-pointing mountain. One recognizes here that
Dante, in spite of his theological and philosophical sophis-
tication, is incapable of taking the natural world for
granted. In other words, his immense learning and profoundly intellectual disposition do not drown out the won-
derment of the new man waking to first awareness of sun,
moon, rivers, oceans, hills. This is where myth began. And
in his exposition of the light in Purgatory Dante never
loses hold on the enduring element in mythic feeling—that
primary awe in the presence of a great cosmic force felt
as the agent of an active, yet secret and mysterious will.

That primary wonder is not present in the texts of the
Christian or pagan philosophers. Nor does one find it in
mediaeval legend; nor, I think, even in the Old Testament, with all its acknowledgments of magnificence in the
creation. In the devotional works the image of light is
drawn upon only to qualify the subject of thought: namely,
God. In the *Comedy* physical light—which ultimately is to
serve the same function—is *there*, present in the scene, an
object of intense wonder, interest and delight. In Hell it is
conspicuously and painfully absent; in the foothills of Purgatory, where its course is followed from hour to hour in
the natural sky, it dominates; gradually, as we climb the
mountain, it is made more and more persuasively transparent, so that its significance in the symbolic order stands
forward with equal force; in the *Paradiso*, raised to higher
and higher powers of beauty and radiance, the visible light
is joined with the exposition of God's action in an open
analogy, until, as the poem ends, what is *seen* is merged
with what is *understood*.

Another tradition, probably as old as thought, gave
Dante the metaphorical identification of *light* with *truth*.
This, which in our time we have so worn out by repetition
that we are no longer aware of what it is we are doing
when we say that we are "in the dark" or that an idea
"dawns" on us, Dante received as fresh and rich, and made
of it the key metaphor governing the whole action of his

story. Somewhat as Plato had done in the Cave Myth (and how hard it is to believe that Dante never knew that text!) he re-creates the metaphorical equation and explores it from Hell to the Empyrean revealing the underlying connection: namely, that the energizing of the eye in the presence of light resembles the energizing of the mind in the presence of truth.

The New Testament and Christian Neoplatonism gave him the final equation in which the two others (God is light; light is truth) are merged: God's wisdom is his light, visible in Christ, who is called the *Word of God*, and is named by John and all who follow him, *The Light*.

Every reader forms his own notion of the germinating centre of Dante's poem. I should place it without question here, in the notion that the creative power which brings the whole universe into being is Absolute Truth, whose action may be conceived under the analogy of its legitimate offspring, the natural light of the sun. Radiant, variable in its penetration, reverberant, such truth is mediated to the human creature; but if he has and uses the organs with which he has been equipped to *see*, he may divine the Source.

Inferno

According to the letter of the text, it is dark in Hell, except where—or better, *even* where tongues of flame or rains of sparks torment certain inhabitants. Cut off from the sun, a region of *eternal shadows, mute of all light*, its air *tenebrous, forever dyed, black as perse*, the river Styx flows through it with *dusky and dirty waves* between *malign gray shores*, and Phlegethon boils red as blood.

Literally, Hell is a cavern under earth in which the souls of impenitent sinners are shut up eternally after death to suffer the penalties of their wrongdoings. Literally it is the dark prison of retribution. But as the poem takes hold on the reader and begins to open out in figurative meaning, it suggests even more cogently that Hell is an image of the means by which the human soul hurts and destroys itself

—the place being fallenness from God, and the suffering nothing else than the bite of the sin itself.

On this second view, the figurative one, the literal dark might seem to imply a withholding of his light by God. But if this were the case, the conception of that light as the ground of truth would become absurd; for if truth could choose to obscure itself, the whole framework of moral meaning in the universe would collapse, and we should be forced back on an interpretation of sin as mere failure to do what the Scriptures or their guardians have enjoined. This, we may easily suspect, is not the case in Dante's thought, so we must ask whether there is anything in the *Inferno* to correct it. Not a word, explicitly. But the defective eyes of the damned suggest an answer. In a *blind world*, we are told, they lead a *blind life;* having been *squint-eyed of mind* on earth, they are now literally to be seen squinting, peering, twisting their eyes awry. It is not the material events at which they strain; for it is evident that they can distinguish every object and action in their immediate proximity, down to the raising of an eyebrow. And they are not deprived of reason. But at one point or another, depending on the desires that have led them here, the sense, the bearings, the connections of things escape them, so that they grasp eagerly for what hurts them. Thus it is in their minds that they are blind—limitedly but persistently—in the area of their own good. They may know the technical reason for their torment, but the real reason eludes them. Nor do they really understand what place they are in.

Now rational blindness, or moral blindness of this sort is, in Dante's view, strictly a human responsibility. The *Inferno* does not state this, however; and thus the reader is free throughout the first book of the *Comedy* to be indignant with God for making some people insufficiently sharp-eyed to steer clear of trouble. He is also free to define the "trouble" as an authoritarian imposition of penalties for arbitrarily designated acts. He is as free, in other words, to "fall" in his reading as the human soul is in its life. But no freer. For if he is alert to the text, he will note its frequent demonstrations that those who are indeed in Hell were, before they fell there, well equipped to see the danger and steer clear of it. (The warning on the gates is a figurative announcement of this unsympathetic fact.) The *Inferno* is a little like Hell itself: easy to get into and very easy to misunderstand. If, however, one reads it through (as, if one escapes damnation), the more difficult purgatorial experience comes next, ready to shed full clarity on the moral condition. To look ahead into the second canticle for just one instance: halfway up the mount the pilgrim learns that every soul at its inception is furnished with a *light* by which it *may know good and evil*.[3] From this one may infer that each soul has good eyes to begin with—eyes capable of making the basic moral distinctions. Furthermore, he comes into a world flooded with the light of absolute truth, which his eyes if they are in working order will reflect. This light cannot fail. Its receptors, however, can. They can turn from it; they can reflect it weakly, or colour it with the hue of their own passions. The very word *reflection*, with its literal and metaphorical senses, is explanatory of the way in which Dante's meaning evolves. For, the unreflective or muddily reflective mind is "dark" by strict analogy to the darkness of an object which does not reflect light. It is an easy step, if one merely externalizes the interior flaw, to say that such a mind is "in the dark". And this is what Dante has done in imaging Hell as an underground, lightless cavern, not *given* by the heavens, but made by eyes which are dull to light; eyes which cannot distinguish a false apparent good from a true good or locate the source of pain where it actually is, in their freely made choices.

Certainly Dante doesn't think that it is easy to see well in these terms; but his *Inferno* shows that the world is posted with danger signs, warning the traveller to look sharp. Weak, unwilling eyes alone create the potentiality of Hell, and Hell becomes actual as soon as the will yields to the beckoning siren shapes that evil takes. Hell altogether is no more nor less than a concrete projection of

[3] *Purg.* XVI, 74

the spiritual condition of its inmates. Its endless circular movement images the concentration of their will on the ego centre (rather than the God circumference), its pain is the quality of their error, and its darkness their inability to form a clear image of their good.

Dante develops this spiritual eye-malady of the damned throughout the *Inferno*, in a variety of innuendoes. He tells us, for instance, that they know the past and future of the living world, but that the events of the present are hidden from them[4]—thus that even the immediate truths of life surrounding them in time elude them. He lets us see their curious unawareness of one another's plights, their sometimes dream-like indifference to an event occurring within arm's reach. He lets us hear them: they tell their own stories, but they miss the point, never seeing the close connection between *this* suffering and *that* action. What they cannot see is, in every case, the very things that would give meaning to past and future, as well as to their present condition—literally, what exists outside their own immediate scope, what lies beyond their particular ditches: the general shape of the moral universe and where Hell stands in it with respect to other modes of being.

There are of course great differences in the degree to which various sinners distort the image of truth, as we see by the increasing gravity of the torments and the narrowing circles of the three main regions of Inferno as we descend into it. And here Dante expresses by changes in the quality of the literal darkness the ways in which differing loves obscure or discolour the simple light of reason.

Darkness and blindness begin even before the crossing of Acheron—in the entryway to Hell, among the Trimmers and at Charon's ferry. They are suspended, however, in the puzzling, troubling interpolation of Limbo. In Limbo there is a fire—the only one in Hell to which Dante assigns a luminous power—that "conquers a hemisphere of the darkness"; and a palace set in a "place open, luminous and high". The people who have won this underground brightness are the ancient sages and heroes of the classical West.

[4] Canto X, 100 ff.

That Dante held them in the highest possible reverence is
plain here, as wherever he refers to them, yet the light and
lofty eminence on which he places them does not mitigate
for any reader the bitter fact that they *are* in the underground prison hemmed in by darkness, walls and river,
remote from the dazzling, free-moving outer spheres of
their universe. It is not only the reader who feels the bitterness of this: the pilgrim, when he reaches the more
thoughtful later stage of his experience, is saddened and
baffled by it, and tries to get Heaven to explain why these
men should be cut off from bliss. Dante knew and felt that
the human creative faculties, reason and imagination, had
never since reached as lofty a development as in these
poets and philosophers. The light of their intelligence was
such that even in remoteness from God (who had not yet
revealed himself to fallen man) they seemed to have come
very close to grasping the ultimate truth. They had taught
the young Christian world how to think, and often what
to think and feel. But Christianity affirms that the only
bridge to God is a light of a totally different order from
theirs, and that this is not implanted in the soul, as is the
germ of moral reason, but given by grace. Those who died
before Christ entered the world to show the way to God
and to wipe out Adam's terrible bequest could do no more
than guess at the existence of some such light. And if any
received it—as did the Emperor Trajan and Trojan Ri-
pheus, according to the *Comedy*[5]—they were recipients of
an exceedingly rare and unpredictable gift. Why, and by
what special miracle, an individual pagan here and there
achieved faith in the Redemption that lay still ahead of
him in time, we do not know and cannot ask. Homer,
Virgil, Plato and their great companions had no such
vision in time, and therefore cannot have it in eternity.
This saddens the pilgrim, moved by his individual love
for them. But the poet, with his unfailing gift for the large
perspective, seems less troubled by their personal loss than
awed by the marvel of their light-giving unenlightenment.

[5] *Par.* XX, 44–45, 67–69, 100 ff.

Statius' words to Virgil much later in the poem ring back over the whole scene:

> *"Facesti come quei che va di notte,*
>   *che porta il lume dietro e sè non giova,*
>   *ma dopo sè fa le persone dotte,*
> . . . . ."

"Thou didst like one who goes by night and carries the light behind him, and profits not himself, but maketh persons wise that follow him . . ."

Purg. XXII, 67–69

Past Limbo and throughout the first major division of Hell, the Incontinent languish in a simple, unembellished semi-darkness.[6] Their sin is an excessive love for objects which were not without merit of love. The external darkness of their place, the mere absence of *anything that shines*, of all brightness and of any colours but black, grey and brown, coupled with what the narrative reveals about them, defines their vision as an obscuring of the truth, but not a distorting of it. The Incontinent do not see clearly enough to recognize the point at which their loves begin to outrage reason and lead inevitably to suffering.

When we come to the second of the three great divisions of Inferno, beginning at the walls surrounding the City of Dis,[7] the darkness is for the first time varied—by fire-light and fire colour. Twin beacons spring up in a high tower, red *mosques* appear, coloured by "the eternal fire that causes them to glow within". And here, under the earth roof, beside the filthy stream, begins one of the most hazardous and curious episodes of the whole canticle. Because it reveals a good deal about the powers and limitations of rational vision, a close view of it may be worth pausing for.

The two who stand outside the gates of Dis, are in the literal story, a young man who has blundered his way into

---

[6] This remark is very summary indeed. For an absorbing study of Dante's pictorial and figurative use of light, shadow and colour throughout the *Comedy*, the reader is referred to Guido di Pino, *La Figurazione della Luce nella Divina Commedia* (Florence 1952).   [7] VIII, 67 ff.

a spiritual *impasse* and the shade of an old poet surpass-
ingly gifted with rational wisdom and love. In their allegorical figures—and here I repeat the deduction of most of
Dante's interpreters—they are the simple human soul and
the rational mind which is instinctively dear to that soul.
The guardians of Dis who come out to bar their way are
more than a thousand angry spirits *rained from heaven*—
angels who fell with Lucifer, thus not souls at all, but intelligences inimical to light. They attempt to dismiss the
living man, alone, and to hold Virgil prisoner; which, were
they to succeed, would end the guidance of reason, and so
the voyage, leaving the pilgrim worse off than he had been
in the Dark Wood. By command, then by threat, they try
to separate the living soul from his irreplaceable rescuer.
Why? Because Virgil is a light-supplier and they are the
light-deniers. If this duo of travellers persists, the one will
imbibe more and more light until he outdistances the
other and stands at the place from which they fell. They
fell because they chose to. They are "for" Hell and for the
dark. Thus their natural interest is to hold souls in it. Hell
is a trap and not a pass to heaven, such as Virgil would
make of it for his pupil.

They do not succeed in separating the two. But although, Virgil refuses to quit the pilgrim, the first phase
of the attempt to enter Dis ends in failure and terror: the
gates are closed against the travellers, and Virgil is for the
moment baffled. Three Furies appear now on the high
walls and shout for the Medusa to come and turn the living man to stone. Virgil's instructions to his charge at
this point are very interesting: the pilgrim is to turn his
back and close his eyes, "for if the Gorgon show herself
and thou shouldst see her, there would be no returning
up again." Then, as though he could trust only himself in
so delicate a matter, he turns the younger poet around and
places his hands over the endangered eyes. This is a startling moment for the reader—in part because of the sense
of fearful danger suggested in Virgil's actions and looks,
and in part because of the very queerness of this threat,
offered as it is to the hero of a Christian pilgrimage by

an outmoded mythic demon, and accepted with all serious-
ness. And Dante wants the reader to stop and question
what this may mean. He breaks into the action to speak
in his own voice: "O ye who have sane intellects, mark
the doctrine which conceals itself beneath the veil of the
strange verses!"[8]

We are not to take the allegory any less seriously because it is here using stock figures from the book of myth.
Nor can we explain the Medusa by her good theatricality;
for Dante never outrages sense in such a way. The Medusa
has the reality of the Furies, the centaurs, the demons of
the *Inferno*—all original creations of the mythic imagination, which Dante regarded as mistaken only in assigning
a specific and separate existence to the forces it identified
in this way. The forces are real enough in any world, however it may have exploded the myths. And in an image of
Hell, whose entire substance is a concretization of states
of mind, and where every dark thing that has been dredged
up from man's psyche has its proper place, their mytho-
logical bodies are perfectly proper to the scene. The Medusa is actually there at the walls of Dis, and capable, if
not of turning a man to stone, of preventing (as Virgil
says) his "returning up again". The reality of the Medusa
is there, too—that pure essence of the irrational, whose
action is to freeze the human will, to annul it altogether,
cutting it away from reason. The Medusa is what the
White Whale was to Captain Ahab:

> All that most maddens and torments; all that stirs up
> the lees of things, all truth with malice in it; all that
> cracks the sinews and cakes the brain; all the subtle
> demonisms of life and thought.[9]

That is why Virgil, everywhere else so intent on having
his pupil see all there is to be seen, tells him here to do
the only thing that can save a man in such circumstances:
namely, to shut his eyes and cover them over. And the
doctrine of the strange verses appears to be that the human creature has no recourse whatever against the venom

8 IX, 61–63   9 H. Melville, *Moby Dick*, chap. XLI

of the irrational—none in fortitude and surely none in argument—except to avoid the encounter altogether.

Yet only half the battle is won by Virgil. Dante has put it that human reason can stand pat against the irrational and guard the psyche against the fatal meeting, but not that it can subdue an enemy of this order. What is required to dispel the Medusa is not Virgil's little incandescence but a light equivalent in force to the Medusa's powerful darkness. In the framework of the poem this means another imaginary embodiment of a real essence. It means, specifically, that the assertive power of truth must manifest itself. In such roles Dante casts his unfallen angels—creatures of pure light, as we shall learn in the *Paradiso*. At the gates of Dis the angel comes in a crash of sound that shakes both shores, a *messenger of heaven* of whom we see nothing except that he passes the Stygian ferry *with soles unwet* and waves the gross air from before his face in a single contemptuous gesture. The enemy flee like frogs. The poets enter Dis without further obstacle.

That Dis is the city of fire we learn from Farinata[10] as soon as we have entered. The central burning, however, is never made visible; instead, it breaks out here and there as though bursting from the air and the ground. It appears as *scattered flames* in the tombs of the Heretics, it is sensed under the river of blood that boils the company of the Violent-against-their-fellows[11]; undoubtedly it parches the earth in which the Suicides take root, for in the following round it falls in *dilated flakes of fire* on the Violent-against-God, Nature and Art. No colour or brightness is attributed to these flames. The waters alone are ruddy: Phlegethon's tributary, *a little rivulet the redness of which still makes me shudder*, quenches the flames where it passes, giving a pathway to the pilgrims until they reach the upper rim of Malebolge.

In Malebolge the fire is seen far less often. It plays over the upturned feet of the Simonists, is guessed under the stewing pitch of the Barrators, consumes certain Thieves, and envelops the Evil Counsellors in cocoons of flame. Then it vanishes altogether.

The reader is left to interpret the fire of Dis for himself, according to his inferences, for the pilgrim still understands too little to grasp the meaning of the things he sees with such fortunate objective clarity, and he is either too intent or too moved to ask questions of Virgil. Obviously desire plays a part in this burning of the abyss. But desire alone, however great, is an insufficient explanation, since every sentient creature—not to single out the Incontinent, who lie above and outside the City of Fire—is moved by desire. It is the difference in rational light among the several clans of Hell which is the real determinant. For the Incontinent, who have simply abandoned reason (in the sense of "subjecting it to desire"), are prisoned in *obscurity*, pure and simple. But the Violent and the Fraudulent, down as far as Cocytus, far from abandoning reason, use it and deform it by the interpenetration of their desire: all down the descent they are increasingly deliberate in their action. Thus Dante pictures them as existing in the ruddy false-light of their concealed fire, or in the momentary gleam of its outbreaking sparks and flames. In them the burning of desire throws the distorting shadow of the self across the clear image of things as they are. The towers are red, the rivers are red, showers of sparks fall on the Sandy Plain, the Valley of the Evil Counsellors flashes like a hillside covered with fireflies.

All of Dis burns; we must assume this from Virgil's reference to an eternal fire that inflames the lower Hell and colours its towers,[12] as well as from Farinata's phrase, *the city of fire*. If many of the Fraudulent appear to stand free of the fire, we must still suppose that, in that City, they see according to its discoloured light. From the first round of Dis (the Heretics) to the last of Cocytus, we are witnessing a progressive corruption of human reason, first by love directed to the wrong goals, and in the final circle by love shrunken and retracted in the cold mind of the traitor poised for his single deed.

[12] VIII, 73–74

In a very simple sense the fact that the Fraudulent burn without appearing to, is exactly what we ought to expect: frauds not only show a cool face to the world, but frequently do so to themselves as well, convinced while they burn that they are stirred only by the most elevated motives. (Surely Dante must have had some such thought in mind when he found Mahomet, Tiresias, Manto among his Fraudulent.)

In an equally simple sense it is right that Cocytus be plunged in ice. In this circle of Traitors, where the mind does its worst work, we feel the deadly coldness of deliberation following after passion but putting passion aside, under cover. We are now as far as possible from the sun, infinitely far from the source of wisdom, with love sealed down under the frozen element. If there is light here, it is white with the dead pallor of the ice—of intellect working altogether without heart, and burning cold.

The poor vision of the damned in this last circle is complicated by their immobility. The sin of treachery is felt as possessing the whole mind, making it incapable of the slightest variation in range. So rigidly is the gaze of these damned fixed on the objective of their terrible concern that the mere bending of a neck to look upward—which means to look at something new, at other folk—is a painful effort against the grip of the ice; and momentary tears freeze the eyes into blindness again immediately.[13] The imprisonment of the sinners in the ice which cauterizes all their sensibilities is progressively greater as we move inward towards the narrow centre of the earth; the last group of Traitors, those who betrayed their lords and benefactors, frozen into the lake like straws, can neither see nor hear nor move. Followers of Lucifer, traitors to the absolute light which endowed them with some of its own qualities, their idleness, darkness and coldness are the ultimate and total betrayal of God's creative power, light and love.

The pilgrim does not escape infection. Set down on the lake of ice by the giants he looks back rather than around,

13 XXXII, 40–50; and see above, p. 175.

and does not even see what the new place is until someone underfoot cries out to him. All his interest is centred on getting a roster of names: he abuses and tricks the dead into revealing the identities they want to hide, seizing one by the hair of the head, and bribing another with promise of an act of mercy which he then refuses to perform. He passes through the four concentric rounds of the ice without any but a superficial and almost vicious awareness of plight, busy but unreflective, and scarcely attentive to the more and more silent Virgil. It is Virgil who compels him to look up when they near the centre, and to see Satan feature by feature, and then half guides half carries him— he is by this time *neither alive nor dead*—away from Hell, out of the dark tunnel, *to see the stars again*.

Purgatorio

Dolce color d'oriental zaffiro,
  che s'accoglieva nel sereno aspetto
  del mezzo, puro insino al primo giro,

alli occhi miei ricominciò diletto,
  tosto ch'io usci' fuor dell'aura morta
  che m'avea contristati li occhi e 'l petto.

Sweet hue of orient sapphire which was gathering on the clear forehead of the sky, pure even to the first circle,

to mine eyes restored delight, soon as I issued forth from the dead air which had afflicted eyes and heart.

I, 13–18

The images of natural light flooding the *Purgatorio* with brilliance, colour and energy are as euphoric to the reader who comes to them from the dark, menacing forms of Hell as is the actual renewal of the light to the glad pilgrim who notices and records where the sun stood in the sky at every pause or change in his long journey, what stars appeared and where they hung with respect to the horizon, what moonlight and what shadows. He is unable

to forget that the sun is present and real, dawning over
Purgatory as it sets on the Ganges, or near it; nor that
he has left the dimension of a cursed eternity and entered
into time again—but good time, time graced by the place
he is in, since it measures the *diritta via*, and leads where
one truly wills to go.

He sees the visible markers of time with astonished
fresh eyes. And some sense of their pristine beauty and
animation is given to the reader in the verses that restore
their mythologic names and roles.

> *La concubina di Titone antico*
> *già s'imbiancava al balco d'oriente,*
> *fuor delle braccia del suo dolce amico.*

> *di gemme la sua fronte era lucente,*
> *poste in figura del freddo animale*
> *che con la coda percuote la gente.*

Now was the concubine of ancient Tithonus at eastern terrace growing white, forth from her sweet lover's
arms.

with gems her forehead was glittering, set in the form
of the cold animal that strikes folks with its tail.

IX, 1–6

> *L'alba vinceva l'ora mattutina*
> *che fuggìa innanzi . . .*

The dawn was vanquishing the breath of morn that
fled before her . . .

I, 115

> *Da tutte parti saettava il giorno*
> *lo sol, ch'avea con le saette conte*
> *di mezzo il ciel cacciato Capricorno.*

On every side the sun, who with his arrows bright
had chased the Goat from midst of heaven, was shooting forth the day.

II, 55–57

With the natural light colour, too, floods the poem: in green grass, green wings, white marble, gold and silver keys, flowers that surpass

> *Oro e argento fine, cocco e biacca,*
>   *indaco, legno lucido, sereno,*
>   *fresco smeraldo in l'ora che si fiacca.*

gold and fine silver, cramoisy and white, indian wood bright and clear, fresh emerald at the moment it is split.

VII, 73–75

Smiling planets, the walking feet of Night, Aurora breathing and turning pale, and the constant procession of the sun up and down the sky: these are the adornments of the natural light, seen with primal and innocent eyes. As Francis Fergusson makes clear in his study of the pilgrim's education in Purgatory, the first day on the mountain is above all one of childlike and lyric perception, deep, "but without understanding" and "associated with the poetry of the race, the heritage of myth".[14]

The heritage of myth is invoked throughout the poem. For the myth-makers, as we have observed before, were in Dante's view not altogether wrong, although they reached the wrong conclusions; and their approximations contain what the first impulse of love and awe towards the natural world must catch sight of: the god mirrored there. The Muses are the patrons of the poet writing his vision of the Terrestrial Paradise, and Apollo that of the whole third canticle. Actually, neither the lyric yearning nor the mythic personifications disappear as the voyager moves on to acquire his deeper insights. Rather, new ways of seeing are added to the old and simpler ones of the first childlike day. So that always, underlying the moral and metaphysical symbolism of sun and stars, we shall continue to find the light given as palpable colour, shape, motion, and as the felt but unreasoned presence of the

[14] Francis Fergusson, *Dante's Drama of the Mind* (Princeton Univ. Press, 1953), chap. II.

god. *Handmaiden* hours stand in the sky assisting constellations in their changes; the planet Venus burns *with fire of love*; Aurora's cheeks change colour as the day grows. Not only is the canticle shot through with living light and colour by such passages, and the reader insistently reminded by them of the beauty of shifting light and shade on earth, but their constant pressure on the key of beauty and order in the daily round of light instils into the texture of the poem an exultancy, a sense of the miraculous in the familiar, which is never dimmed away by the hardships of the climb, the views of penitential suffering, or the philosophic discourses. Dante believes that the miraculous *is* present in such familiar things—and not by chance, but because the created universe resembles and expresses its divine source.

At sunset of the first day the metaphysical connections of the natural light begin to make themselves apparent. But although they are broached in a supernatural event, the touch is light, and the pilgrim is set to wondering only briefly, without grasping the significance of what he hears. Virgil has asked Sordello, with whom the two have stopped to talk at some length, to point out the upward path, so that he and his pupil may get on with their journey. Sordello answers that they had better choose a resting place for the night where they are, since the sun is about to set and no mounting upward will be possible after that:

> E 'l buon Sordello in terra fregò 'l dito,
>   dicendo: "Vedi, sola questa riga
>   non varcheresti dopo il sole partito:
>
> non però ch'altra cosa desse briga
>   che la notturna tenebra ad ir suso:
>   quella col non poder la voglia intriga."

And the good Sordello drew his finger across the ground, saying, "Look, even this line thou wouldst not cross after the sun is set:

not for that aught else than the darkness gave hindrance to going upward: that hampers the will with lack of power."

VII, 52–57

The poet does not offer any explanation of this extraordinary state of things, and the commentators are apt to dismiss it with a conjecture to the effect that the sun here signifies divine grace. The reader, faced with the awesome doctrine and the strict ban announced by Sordello, may easily feel here that the *Comedy* is abandoning him to a magic formula, a control over spiritual destiny which appears to have no correspondence in human experience. But this is not the case.

In the sunset events on Purgatory we see that the individual will, while it is the only force required to take the soul up from one scarp to the next, cannot act except under the conditions of clear vision. Sordello has told the travellers plainly that it is darkness alone which will hold them back, by hampering the will with impotence. He means, I should say, that it is impossible to enter into the process of moral discipline blindly; every step of such a road must be fully visible and fully comprehended. In showing this to us Dante himself makes no reference to any dogma or doctrine of the Church, however plainly one may seem implied. He tells us that the mind which is geared to its task, but needs more light than it inherently possesses, eventually gets that light. The principle underlying this conviction (the same one that brought forth the saving angel at the entry into Dis) is clear and simple: namely, the affirmative power of truth.

But there is something else that Dante is perhaps even more interested in making us aware of at this point in the narrative. He points out to us a distinction between the condition of full repentance (the general option against sin and for the good) which brings a soul inside the gates of Purgatory, and the energy of intelligence and will required to propel him upward against the gravity of the world's contrary attraction. He shows that it is not an auto-

matic effect of penitence that one achieves Heaven—
which is to say, that one becomes proof against sin and
possessed of virtue. Neither the mountain nor virtue is as
simple as that. One cannot arrive at the final goal by even
the purest determination to be good, alone: one must will
not only the general objective, but every successive step of
the way. But each step of Purgatory involves suffering; and
if this, which is contrary to nature, is to be willed, the
soul must have a rare degree of clarity with respect to it:
that perfect clarity which would make the pain not merely
endurable, but longed for. And one must find one's own
way: there are no escorts, and the paths are not marked.
A very full view of virtue and sin is required to meet these
conditions.

The sun provides this.

The sun, like God for whom it is here the surrogate
figure, sheds light, warmth, energy (corresponding to the
wisdom, love and power of God) into the universe so that
each creature may receive according to its kind and disposition. Of these gifts light is, in Dante's view, the supreme
one for man, in the sense that it opens the way for love—
for love bad or good, concupiscent or charitable—rather
than, as is usually supposed, deriving from it.[15] On the
mountain we see that what is physical illumination for the
eye, is intelligence of—and the concomitant real desire for
—the way of purgation. For this mere human light and
desire are (as most postulants for goodness at one time or
another feel) simply not enough.

In Purgatory the will is always open to the light (that
is, always wills to understand), but must sometimes pa-
tiently suffer the relative darkness of the starry nights. On
the other hand, unlike the living man in his enforced
darknesses, the night-time soul on the mountain is assured
that his waiting will be rewarded: the sun *will* come up,
the conditions of sufficient understanding will be given.
This does not mean that he will be able to race uphill
from dawn to the next sunset; the process of achieving

---

15 ". . . affection followeth on the act that doth conceive . . .",
Par. XXIX, 139. And see above, p. 137, n.

enough insight and love to buoy one upward from terrace to terrace is slow or quick according as the soul is weighted by old habits of inattention or of ego-centred love. It has taken Statius almost thirteen centuries to reach the sixth Terrace, while Forese Donati has covered the same distance in four years. But this does not weigh against Statius, nor for Forese. What occurs under the downpouring sun of Purgatory is such a quickening of each soul in that love of the good which it already wills, that it can of its own accord mount the difficult steps from wherever it may stand to whatever lies above, and can freely and joyously undertake such disciplines as it requires and for so long as it feels necessary in order to become perfect in the virtue it had come there to find. To be slow or swift is all one; to be on one's way is what really matters.

Heaven exercises no constraint at all on the human will. Late in the canticle Statius will make it clear to the pilgrim that the whole action of purgation is voluntarily begun and ended, according as the individual soul recognizes first its need for one or another of the disciplines, and then its cure. Each soul offers itself freely to the torments and meditations of such terraces as can heal it of some warping left by past sin. When it completes its work on any terrace, reaching the point where temptation is annulled and the habit of virtue locked in place—the soul itself makes this recognition by rising and moving onward. The magnificence of its achievement is hailed by a general quaking of the whole mountain and a concerted cry of *gloria* from every soul at every stage of the way, acknowledging a truly voluntary act, an act of clear choice resulting, not from a mere impulse to move on, to go somewhere else, but from a perfect possession of the virtue of the quitted terrace and perfect clarity with respect to what lies ahead. And the sun streaming over each such act signifies both the fact and nature of the illumination.

Such symbols do not make the real landscape of Purgatory any less real. The sun, the constellations, the harsh rock of the mountain with its spiral of open passageways and its seven terraces, are solidly there, although they shimmer now with extended meaning. Each entity in a firm present landscape contains both reminders of the living world, and at the same time clues to the moral scene. Thus the sunset of the first day, which is seen and felt as an event of the physical light, there in Purgatory, at once fills the pilgrim with nostalgic memories[16] and reveals itself to him as an event of prime importance in his acquisition of spiritual light.

The pilgrim's shadow is another simple, "real" clue to that other, the moral scene. It is a natural enough phenomenon, and the joy of souls who are able to recognize him as a living man because he casts this shadow seems dramatically apt. But this shadow, so often the object of delighted attention, is nonetheless the one spot of darkness cast on the mountain road by any of its travellers. The souls are translucent; the light enters and passes through them; they are inundated, as it were, by a clarity which the heavy human hide impedes.

The four bright stars that the pilgrim sees rising with the sun at dawn of his first day, and the three which take their place in the night sky, are somewhat more baldly another set of symbol-clues. Visible when the sun is not in the sky, their brightness absorbed by day in the greater brightness, they suggest that even in the absence of the sun's full illumination the soul has guardian lights to see by. The four stars seen before the sun rises easily suggest the four cardinal virtues distinguished by man in the half-light that preceded the Christian day; by a similar analogy, the other three may be taken to represent faith, hope and charity, presiding over the human soul when the divine light, having shed its direct radiance, is temporarily withdrawn.

There is another sort of luminous presence in Purgatory which differs from sun, shadow and stars in that the natural world offers no counterpart to its existence. This is the company of angels—intelligences formed of pure light, and made visibly manifest, as I have suggested earlier, only by a certain poetic licence. There are four angels in the Ante-

16 VIII, 1–6

purgatory, and eight in Purgatory proper, almost all so resplendent that the mortal eye is dazed by them *like a faculty which by excess is confounded.* The *Paradiso* will explain angels; here they are simply *given*—but given with such conviction of their being that the reader will no more question their winged and robed and articulate manifestation than the pilgrim does.

In the Antepurgatory:

> *Verdi come fogliette pur mo nate*
> *erano in veste, che da verdi penne*
> *percosse traean dietro e ventilate.*

. . . . .

> *Ben discernea in lor la testa bionda;*
> *ma nella faccia l'ocohio si smarrìa,*
> *come virtù ch'a troppo si confonda.*

Green as tender leaves just born was their raiment, which they trailed behind, fanned and smitten by green wings.

. . . . .

Clearly I discerned the fair hair of them, but in their faces the eye was dazed like a faculty which by excess is confounded.

VIII, 28–36

At the stairway to the second Terrace:

> *A noi venìa la creatura bella,*
> *bianco vestito e nella faccia quale*
> *par tremolando mattutina stella.*

To us came the beauteous creature robed in white, and in his countenance such as a tremulous star at morn appears.

XII, 88–90

The angel of temperance:

> *Drizzai la testa per veder chi fossi;*
> *e già mai non si videro in fornace*
> *vetri o metalli sì lucenti e rossi,*

com'io vidi un che dicea: "S'a voi piace
  montare in su, qui si conven dar volta;
  quinci si va chi vuole andar per pace."

L'aspetto suo m'avea la vista tolta.

I raised my head to see who it was, and never in a
furnace were glasses or metals seen so glowing and
red

as I saw one who said: "If it please you to mount upward, here must a turn be given; hence goeth he who
desires to go for peace."

His countenance had bereft me of sight.

XXIV, 136–142

Enough has been said about the divine light streaming
through Purgatory so that little need be added about angels. A part of the formal ritual of the ordered and ordering mountain, one of them stands to hail the travellers at
the end of every terrace. Their words praise, with the
appropriate Beatitude, the virtue just acquired, their wing-
beat signals the lifting away of the sin just cancelled, and
their personal blaze gives additional light to the sunlit
passageways. The final terrace, alone, has a pair of these
birds divine, stationed one on the hither, one on the far
side of the curtain of flame that lines the inner wall and
offers the final disciplinary torment. The first of these angels speaks the Beatitude in praise of chastity, and hails
into the fire all those who come to burn lust away. The
other—who appears at first unidentified and supernumer-
ary—invites across the flames all those, without exception,
who reach this place, tainted or not with lust, and who
are headed for the final mountain station, the Terrestrial
Paradise.

The second angel and his strict command (*No farther
may ye go, O hallowed souls, if first the fire bite not; enter
therein . . .*) are not explained other than by the action
itself. The reader is expected either accurately to feel, or
else to puzzle out for himself why it is that every soul,

however complete in human virtues, must pass through the flames. He is expected to observe that the fire of the seventh Terrace has two separate but related functions: all along the curve from the first to the second angel, it is a crucible for lust and a therapy in fraternal love; while, at the point where the second angel stands guard, it is a burning bridge, for all souls, between discrete mortal attachments and the love of God.

The extraordinary appropriateness and subtlety of this arrangement does not immediately make itself felt, for this is one of those passages in which Dante's imagery undoubtedly grows out of a learned pondering. But if one reads it along with St Augustine's teaching concerning covetousness, the probable course of Dante's thought— and with it the life of his image—are revealed in dimensions one had not even suspected earlier.

St Augustine says, in effect, that *concupiscentia* is the opposite of *caritas*, but that both have a single source in *amor*.[17] His reference here is to concupiscence in its wide sense, as all possessive creature-love; and he opposes it to that totally selfless love of God in which all particular loves are transmuted. Now, every sin that the mountain obliterates is a portion of *concupiscentia* in this wide sense. Every virtue replacing a cancelled sin is a portion of *caritas*. And when all the sins have been cancelled and all the virtues firmly possessed, every impediment to *caritas* is done away with, and the soul is, as it were, impelled forward from its piecemeal love of the good into a single and undivided love of a single and indivisible good. The entry of souls into the flame of the passageway signifies this fusion of many loves in perfect *caritas*.

But concupiscence has also a restricted sense—the more familiar one, according to which it means overweening

[17] "Love is covetousness (*concupiscentia*) when the creature is loved for its own sake; and then it serves not to aid our use but to corrupt our enjoyment." But "a love of the creature, if it be referred to the Creator, becomes charity (*caritas*) and not covetousness". St Augustine, *The Trinity*, Bk. IX, sec. 12; edited and tr. by John Burnaby in *Library of Christian Classics*, vol. VIII (Westminster Press, 1955).

sexual desire. In this narrower sense it is the final sin to
be undone in Purgatory and replaced by its opposite,
namely, chastity. And this means, not chastity in the sense
of lust restrained, but in the proper sense of lust absent
in the presence of love. Thus conceived, chastity is no
longer a merely negative, privationary state. And as a positive, as a way of loving, we can see that it is related to
caritas as lust is to the more inclusive *concupiscence*. We
can see also that there is no real paradox in imaging chastity as a flame, and can understand why the seventh Terrace burns the Lustful, instead, say, of cooling them. It
fights a blinding, limited fire with a luminous comprehen-
sive one, and brings the soul that has already cast out
every other possessive leaning to the point where it knows
and therefore can command the flesh.

What nicer statement of the case, then, than to unite
the two functions of the fire of *caritas* in one bank of
flame with successive and related effects: first (in the terrace circle, which is for the Lustful, alone), making every
covetous love chaste; and next (in the passageway, which
is for all souls upward bound), setting every chaste love
blazing in the love of the One?

Terrace fire and the fire of the City of Dis recall one
another. They must do so, for they are counterparts, with
respect to the quality as well as to the object of the loves
they signify. The one on an open mountaintop, in the sunlight, free-mounting and unimpeded, burning with desire
and understanding directed outward towards the absolute
Good and absolute Truth; the other underground, in the
dark, burning with desire and intelligence directed inward,
towards that point *to which all weights converge:* towards
the self.

Through all of these experiences—the simple refresh-
ment of natural, primal light, the sun's literal and figurative illumination of the road and its suffusion of vigour
and love, the view of angels burning in their own chaste
fires—the pilgrim climbs Purgatory in his own way, finding
out by observation, questioning, thinking, feeling, dream-

ing and imaginative inspiration what the good of the soul is, and how attained.

He is all eyes from the moment the mists of Hell are bathed from his face at Cato's orders. His vision is so quickened in the *light*[18] of Virgil, who *guides his eyes on high*,[19] that he seizes easily the difficult teachings which come to him in answer to his increasingly keen questioning. He climbs the mountain *to be blind no longer*,[20] and does in fact acquire here *the keen eyes of the mind*.[21] All day long he studies the action of the penitential terraces, questioning the souls and becoming more and more alert to the significances revealed in what he sees. At night, when the climbing is interrupted, he turns to Virgil and Statius for glosses that fill up the hours before sleep. His prophetic dreams before dawn reveal to him something of the bent of his own mind. And his problems—his individual sin of pride, his political factionalism, his bitterness—are progressively resolved.

His whole journey is penetrated by metaphors of light describing every act of understanding as one of vision, and all positive truth in terms of illumination. Beatrice is promised him as *a light between truth and intellect*,[22] ethical reason is described as *a light given you to know good and evil*[23]; the imagination is set in motion by a light which *takes its form in heaven, of itself, or by a will that sendeth it down*.[24] Finally, the lofty light from which all lesser lights are kindled is that *good* which *speedeth so to love as a ray of light comes to a bright body*.[25] And thus a beginning is made of the image of God's action as it is to be developed throughout the *Paradiso*.

The pilgrim's whole achievement is an earning of light, a cure of his eyes in rational understanding, and a beginning of *caritas*. He has not yet got that equal weight of love for the Good which moves the penitent souls, but with his present insights and the love with which he begins to burn in the passageway to the Garden, he can

[18] XVIII, 10–11   [19] XXI, 124   [20] XXVI, 38
[21] XVIII, 16–17   [22] VI, 45   [23] XVI, 75
[24] XVII, 17–18   [25] XV, 68

hardly again fall into the world's familiar traps. It is this that Virgil understands when he says to him in farewell:

> "*Libero, dritto e sano è tuo arbitrio,*
> *e fallo fora non fare a suo senno:*
>
> *per ch'io te sovra te corono e mitrio.*"

"Free, upright and whole is thy will, and 'twere a fault not to act according to its prompting;

wherefore I do crown and mitre thee over thyself."
                                        XXVII, 140–142

Crowned and mitred (for the world, not for Heaven), having ranged as far as Virgil's eyes *of themselves can discern*, he is now ready for what Beatrice alone can guide him towards: the perception of absolute truth, beyond the stretch of intellect.

He enters the Terrestrial Paradise still human, still limited; a mental traveller who grasps with understanding and desire that perfect moral carriage which the souls who have climbed the mountain take with them in easy possession.

Paradiso

The third canticle is the supreme test of Dante's poetic power, since here he faces the virtually impossible task of making the concrete world of images suggest an experience which is totally foreign to almost every reader, and which, by its very nature, would seem untranslatable into words. It is a supreme test of the reader, too: if he is honest, he will see that the book has no easy charm; he must give it the severest attention before he can come to its severe and radiant beauty. He must lay aside altogether the comforting vain little joke about the boredom of the eternal hosannas of Heaven as compared with the liveliness of Hell. Lastly, if he have not yet *lifted up his neck for bread of angels*, he must wish to try.

As for the critic, all persons who write or talk about the *Paradiso* must not merely take heed of Dante's perfectly serious warning to those who try to follow him in little skiffs[26]—which is warning with regard to the high sense of the poem—but must, whatever the size of their craft, beware of pursuing a poetic effect as though it were a murderer at large. For it is one thing to shoot a desperado, and another to make an interesting corpse of so living and resistant a work of art. I give notice that I am aware of these dangers; and, being perhaps about to fall into the trap (when all I mean to do is to report certain facts), I warn the reader duly. Let him keep the text of the *Paradiso* in his hand; it has for over six hundred years successfully protected itself against critical shrinkage and deformation.

The pilgrim's voyage in the *Paradiso* is in its simplest sense an effortless rising from sphere to sphere of a concentric, ten-sphered universe, with the earth at centre and the unmoving Empyrean outmost. It is at the same time the travelling of an immaterial path of intellectual light, educating him in the relation of human life to eternal being, and of human judgment to absolute truth; leading him finally to a momentary glimpse of the ordering and limiting principle of all existence, the totally immaterial Goal and Source of all thought and all matter.

But this is far easier to state neatly than truly, for a precision of ideas, if one can reach it, is no more the ideal key to the final poetic experience than to the spiritual transformation Dante is attempting to render. The lovely verb *trasumanar*, a key-word to the canticle, opening and locking at the same time, epitomizes our difficulty: if the poet speaks as one transhumanized, he must borrow and patch up human language to express this state; while the reader, as he grasps the notion of transhumanization, grasps also the fact of his own remoteness from it.

By its imaging process the poem develops this necessary sense of remoteness, with its implicit insights. The literal journey does not, as in the earlier canticles, form a concrete and easily grasped starting point for the steps of the figurative journey. In the *Paradiso* as the goal of the whole

[26] *Par.* II, 1–15.

action is more and more closely approximated to light,
the field of the literal journey thins away into the airiest
remnant of concreteness; the travellers enter into the body
of the moon; they halt on the body of the sun, unscorched;
there is no visible landscape whatever on the planets, and
nothing meets the eye but souls and soul-formations. Furthermore, nothing that is witnessed in Heaven—neither the
appearances of souls nor their motions—corresponds to any
familiar experience. The souls are sparks and torches; they
move in garlands, in cross-form, in eagle-outline. There is
no anchorage in the home world of solid things for these
strange sights. We are lifted from firm ground and set
down on, surrounded by, discoursed to by light. Too much
of it? More variations, embellishments and contradictions
of experience than the reader can take in? But surely no-
body ever knew better than Dante what he risked, as well
as what he stood to gain. Surely he meant to press the
reader beyond the commonplace, saturate him with light,
force him to struggle with it in difficult symbols and inter-
locked analogies, to feel it as energy and delight in the
innumerable splendours, sparklings, whirlings, brighten-
ings, with their musical quality and their dancing motion.
He meant to inundate the reader with images of light until
the incandescence, increased beyond anything that might
be mistaken for mere *visibilia*—the outrageous incandescence—together with all the things seen which could not
possibly be seen by eyes, suggest what they are intended
to mean, and precipitate an intellectual atmosphere filled
with the exultancy of understanding and its consequent
love. We are supposed to understand Beatrice well when
she describes the Empyrean as composed of

> "luce intellettüal, piena d'amore;
> amor di vero ben, pien di letizia;
> letizia che trascende ogni dolzore."

> "light intellectual full-charged with love, love of true
> good full-charged with gladness, gladness which tran-
> scendeth every sweetness."

XXX, 40–42

By the time we reach the final three heavens with their increasingly extraordinary sights, Dante has led us to feel suspended between two kinds of being: cut away from the almost familiar variety in which ideas are couched in matter, and craning forward towards the ideal, where they exist in total independence. Deliberately and gradually he has undone our sense of an abiding metaphor under whose terms we have been able to view alternately two sorts of reality, two sorts of brightness—the one sensible, the other ideal—and has left us with a peculiar new awareness of the two as integrated, absolute, as one thing, perfectly real, but of which we cannot say what thing it is. This entity is what the transhumanized eyes see. It is what the reader is left craning forward towards, with the feeling that the very slightest additional push would precipitate him, too, into it. Dante has led us as close as he could to an approximation of what he understands to be at the heart of existence. How close, how worth following, each reader determines for himself.

Two images based on light—one at the beginning, one close to the end of the canticle—gather up between them and summarize the great theme of God's action, both creative and resumptive, as an eternal shattering of his light into the universe and a gathering back of its reflections from every member of the creation. The first of these images describes the primal issuing of the One into the Many, and governs all the *analyses* of the poem. It is extremely brief:

> La gloria di colui che tutto move
> per l'universo penetra e risplende
> in una parte più e meno altrove.

The glory of him who moves all things penetrates throughout the universe and reglows in one place more and in another less.[27]

I, 1–3

[27] The Carlyle-Wicksteed translation has here been altered to follow the original more exactly.

The second describes the essential interrelationship of all created things and their attributes, celebrating the consummation of universal wholeness in God. It governs the *syntheses* of the poem, and is their final statement. The pilgrim, looking into the absolute light, records this:

> *Nel suo profondo vidi che s'interna,*
> *legato con amore in un volume,*
> *ciò che per l'universo si squaderna;*
>
> *sustanze e accidenti e lor costume,*
> *quasi conflati insieme, per tal modo*
> *che ciò ch'i' dico è un semplice lume.*
>
> *La forma universal di questo nodo*
> *credo oh'i' vidi . . .*

Within its depths I saw ingathered, bound by love in one volume, the scattered leaves of all the universe:

substance and accidents and their relations, as though together fused, after such fashion that what I tell of is one simple flame.

The universal form of this complex I think that I beheld . . .

XXXIII, 85–92

If one reads the opening triplet in the popular mood suggested by Dante's reputation as a "beautiful" poet, it is quite likely that one will pass it with no more than a vague impression that something grand and vaguely pious has been uttered. If, however, one expects something more precise of the terms, they will, without losing the grandeur they possess (in Italian), show that they are clearly chosen and distinguished in a carefully balanced statement, meaningful down to the very order in which the words appear. The *glory* comes first—the radiance of God as logical subject of the whole passage. The all-mover occupies a stirring, yet merely descriptive, attributive clause. The two actions of the glory—*penetrates* and *reglows*—seem at first to balance one another perfectly, each with its modifying phrase, the one expressing the outgoing, the other the return of light; *reglows*, however, is weighted by its position at the end of the line, stopping us for a moment as though the train of thought were completed. The final phrase, which does complete the thought, surprises and challenges, and invites us to ask: why, in what way, by what cause does the reflection from the creation differentiate the light which comes to it without distinction of kind or quantity?

The canticle will be at work above all to answer this. It will revert again and again to all these terms, developing each in a variety of instances; but it will be a poem chiefly concerned with the reflected splendour of the universe. Eventually this opening image will expand over the whole range of the canticle until all its terms and their relations are as acutely felt as they are articulated. They will be felt as celebratory of what is and must remain a mystery, yet, as always with Dante, they themselves will be unfolded with utter lucidity and exquisite precision.

The first simple statement of the *glory* is clarified in the traditional matter of the canticle dealing with the divine mystery by which God produces the plurality of the creation. *He who moves all things* is shown to be in essence Absolute Truth (*that truth . . . beyond which no truth hath range*[28]); in manifestation Absolute Light (*that deep light which in itself is true*[29]); and in action *glory* or radiance. The glory is shown penetrating equably throughout the universe, distinct and yet not separate from God (the *living light* issues in such a way *from its source that it departeth not therefrom*[30]), and emerges more and more clearly as signifying Christ, the Logos or Word of God (the splendour *of that idea which our Sire begets in loving*[31]), until the full radiance of creative energy becomes synonymous with the Son of God.

But the second statement of the opening image is of more than equal weight and of greater expansion in the poem. The *reglow* is the testimony, by light, of God's presence in creatures. It is the reverberation of light from the creation's mirroring of God. The most superb poetry

28 IV, 125–126   29 XXXIII, 54   30 XIII, 55–57
31 XIII, 53–54

of the *Paradiso* arises from Dante's concern with this response of the universe to the light that forms and informs
it. That every least creature furnishes a gleam or a splendour according to its kind and capacity—so that a blade of
wheat and a king testify to the same formative Intelligence
and the same ultimate goal, while their excellence or failure results from the conditions of their receptivity—this is
what the poet feels wherever his eye falls on the pursuit
each creature so painstakingly makes of its own entelechy;
this is what he unfolds in instance after instance, full of
love, pity, wonder and awe. This is the subject he is in love
with. The world points to God, instructs him in God; and
God sends him back again, with certain lessons learned,
into the world.

The whole hierarchy of created things, from angels to
clods, lies somewhere in the light-path, unequally open to
it, according as their substance is of one kind or another,
and, within kinds, of one degree or another of receptivity:

> *Nell'ordine ch'io dico sono accline*
> *tutte nature, per diverse sorti,*
> *più al principio loro e men vicine;*
>
> *onde si muovono a diversi porti*
> *per lo gran mar dell'essere,* . . .

In the order of which I speak all things incline by
diverse lots more near and less unto their principle;

wherefore all move to diverse ports o'er the great sea
of being . . .

I, 109–113

The angelic host receive the light directly, divide it
piecemeal among themselves, and in their reglow shed it
downward and outward into the creation as from *so many
mirrors wherein it breaketh*.[32] And mirrors they are, of
the periscope variety, receiving from above and reflecting
into the world below. Intent forever upon God, the angels
are pure receptacles of light; they contain nothing else, no
medium intervenes between them and their object of con-

---

[32] XXIX, 143–144

templation, they are aware of none of the differentiations of time or space.[33] Indifferent in the same sense as God to where the light falls in its reflection from them, they *make no distinction between one or other tenement*[34] that may be open to receive it.

The souls of the blest, too, stand in the direct path of the light, and *reglow* to the point where nothing else of them but their light is visible: in the seven planetary heavens they are perceptible to the pilgrim's eye only as sparks, torches, splendours. But whereas the angels are composed of light, these are *swathed* with it, each according to its greater or lesser capacity sharing *sweet life, with difference, by feeling more and less the eternal breath.*[35] And while direct intelligence of God is in the angelic being, the souls perceive God as external to themselves, however close, and everywhere deeper and wider than their capacity to scan or plumb. Turned directly towards him, they look into him as into *the veracious mirror which doth make itself reflector of all other things,*[36] and read there accurately whatever the scope of their own vision permits. This is what the soul of St Thomas means when he says to the pilgrim:

> *"Così com'io del suo raggio resplendo,*
> *sì, riguardando nella luce etterna,*
> *li tuoi pensieri onde cagioni apprendo."*

[33] Dante follows Aquinas in his definition of angels: they are, according to the *Convivio*, "substances sejunct from matter, to wit Intelligences." In the same book Dante supposes that Plato had the angels in mind when he postulated his Ideas. Plato, he says (II, V, 20 ff.), "laid down not only as many Intelligences as there are movements of heaven, but just as many as there are kinds of things . . . And Plato called them Ideas". If one follows the lead of this reasoning, one will see something of the rationale of angels, and will understand the importance they had for Dante as filling a place which would otherwise have been left vacant in the hierarchy of substances—namely that of pure *act*, free of any potentiality (see *Par.* XXIX, 13–36). I do not mean, however, to overstress the logic of these beings. Their gleaming presences express something further, namely that Truth is otherwise to be perceived as beauty.

[34] VIII, 129   [35] IV, 35–36   [36] XXVI, 103–108

"Even as I glow within its ray, so gazing into the eternal light I apprehend whence thou dost take occasion for thy thoughts."

XI, 19–21

And similarly Cacciaguida to the pilgrim:

". . . i minori e' grandi
di questa vita miran nello speglio
in che, prima che pensi, il pensier pandi."

". . . less and great in this life gaze on the mirror whereon, ere thou thinkest, thou dost outspread thy thought."

XV, 61–63

The God-light when it enters the world, as we have seen, is indirect, reflected down from the angelic receivers, and thus tempered to weak receptacles. Each creature, well-made or poorly such as Nature furnishes it—takes what it can of the proffered light; each makes a fresh *alloy* with it, and *reglows* accordingly. Let men not complain of this differentiation of individuals, for it is not the amount of light he may be able to receive that determines how well a man may live, but his clear or sullied use of it.[37] Great and small minds are found in Hell and Heaven. Further, this differentiation is man's collective boon: because of it man may live *diversely and with diverse offices*,[38] and from the varied human membership create the ordered unity of the state.

Differentiation that resolves itself in unity, unity that gives birth to plurality—this is the way of God (as the two great images beginning and ending the *Paradiso* indicate), and the model followed as nearly as possible by man. The human intelligence divides its single light among the several faculties with which it explores experience; but, too, it strives to unify its perceptions in speculation. Now speculation, as we have already observed, is in Dante's view the supreme function of the human race. And, whether he judges entirely by the distinction this ability

[37] See Piccarda's remarks in III, 70–87.   [38] VIII, 118

confers on man, or in part by the value he, himself, sets on it, Dante's strong sense of order is also pleased to observe that speculation has its divine archetype. How this may be we can see by examining the word *speculation* which proves, like its counterpart, *reflection*, to be a metaphor, and to mean in its literal sense, *mirroring*. Thus the human speculator who begins by mirroring such bits of truth as he may, copies the mirror of all mirrors which captures everything.[39]

Some mortal mirrors are darkened, as we have noted in Hell; but however faint or falsely coloured the light which reglows from these, it is one with that which illuminates the saints. For if *aught else* than the eternal good *seduce your love, naught is it save some vestige of this light, ill understood, that shineth through therein.*[40]

Actually the notion of this single light, everywhere given and everywhere sought after, running along so many strands of thought and action throughout the *Comedy*, is at the heart of the poem's deep life, so that one is false to it to some extent in every schematic or localized discussion. It yields, for example, an acute and profound approach to the tragic quality of man's existence, nowhere stated but built into the whole poem, hint by hint, from the earliest cantos. For we see that man's supreme objective is that unqualified absolute Light which is his source. We see that it was desire for this that engendered his first disobedience and brought about his Fall. In the world he is cut off from it, striving for it. In his notion of truth, which he holds to in his dispossession, and even in pagan ignorance, lies his guarantee that it exists. After long ages of bridgeless remoteness, it has again been made accessible by the Redemption. Yet it is still distant; and man is born with fallible senses and no knowledge of the roads. Material things lure him into their comfortable shadow; they generate the Dark Wood of desire into which he is vir-

[39] It follows that eyes capable of looking at God must see the total contents of all the minor, differently angled mirrors of the creation—and among these the whole history of every mortal mind. So says the great image at the end of the poem. [40] V, 10–12

tually sure to stumble; they generate the three Beasts who, if he cannot circumvent them, will press him by their own paths into the darkest region of all, where he can no longer distinguish the cause of his suffering nor, therefore, cure it. But should he escape the Beasts, he must still pass through Hell and face its dangers in almost naked ignorance, in order to get the first glimmering of the light he so intensely desires and cannot yet locate. And if he emerges (the risk is very great), he must face the arduous purgatorial journey into that submission of self to a power greater than self, which Adam refused, and at which the Old Adam still rebels.

Between the downpouring of the light described in the first lines of the canticle and the gathering of the whole created universe into God at the end, lies the path travelled by Dante's pilgrim, from the condition of moral enlightenment in which he left Purgatory to the instant of transcendent illumination that completes the narrative. His moral education occurred under the light of the natural sun, the *greatest minister of nature, who with the worth of heaven stampeth the world*,[41] displaying to him the practical good—the achievements of making and doing, witnessed in the things done and made there on the mountain. But doing and making are paths; they are undertaken for the sake of something else. If this is so they must come to an end when their goal is reached. And Dante takes this goal to be the perfect understanding that transcends all phenomena, together with its natural consequence of love for that which is understood. The souls of the elect in Paradise have come to the natural end of action, the natural end of their craving for things, and into the possession of them all in flawless contemplation.

The light that fills these souls they reflect willingly upon the living pilgrim. They shower him with discursive lessons, they teach him by their altered and still altering appearances, by their audible harmony and visible grace and ardour, until he begins to know how to winnow the

41 *Par.* X, 28–29

phenomena of space and time for their concealed truths and how to value these on an eternal scale.

Beatrice, too, reflects her light on him. It is by gazing into her eyes and imitating her glance that he rises into the first heaven. With every lesson he masters, because he can see better, more brilliance is made manifest to him in her. She explains this to him in the first sphere:

> "S'io ti fiammeggio nel caldo d'amore
> di là dal modo che 'n terra si vede,
> sì che delli occhi tuoi vinco il valore,
>
> non ti maravigliar; che ciò procede
> da perfetto veder . . ."

"If I flame on thee in the warmth of love, beyond the measure witnessed upon earth, and so vanquish the power of thine eyes,

marvel not; for this proceedeth from perfect vision . . ."

V, 1–5

and adds:

> "Io veggio ben sì come già resplende
> nell' intelletto tuo l'etterna luce . . ."

"Well do I note how in thine intellect already doth reglow the eternal light . . ."

V, 7–8

More and more refulgent until her beauty, which is a transcript of her light, is beyond the poet's ability to describe, Beatrice leads him from sphere to sphere of insight. With every apparent brightening we know that some further film of the human limitation has been lifted from his eyes. In the upper heavens he is blinded three times. The first of these seizures follows his seeing Christ as a *sun* surrounded by the *lamps* of the elect, in the Starry Heaven. Recovering, he records only that he now saw Beatrice with new clarity. Next blinded during his catechism by St John, he is restored by Beatrice and *better than before I saw thereafter*.[42] Finally his vision is dazzled out by the living web of light that surrounds him when he enters the Empyrean; and, recovering, he notes that *there is no such brightness unalloyed that mine eyes might not hold their own with it*.[43]

There comes to his view at once a new sort of vision: a river of light from which emerge living sparks that drop into the cups of flowers along the banks. The sparks are angels; the flowers the redeemed. In this beguiling and surprising figure—which shows the One as a stream, always yet never the same, divided among its own drops and the flowers which these drops beget and nourish—Dante intends a thinning of the already tenuous symbolic mask that separates the pilgrim's mind from essential reality. Yet these appearances, however they enter his new eyes, are still, Beatrice warns, merely *the shadowy prefaces of their reality*.[44] The pilgrim *drinks* the river with his eyes[45]; at once it changes into a rose of light bearing on its petals the hosts of the redeemed visible in yet one more new way. It is impossible for the poet to convey *how* he beheld them. But *as folk under masks seem other than before, if they do off the semblance not their own wherein they hid them*,[46] both angels and the elect are now truly visible.

One must assume that the last of the progressively thinner sensuous appearances of things has here been removed, and that the pilgrim now sees essences without veil. I say we must *assume* this because, while everything points to this, it is a change we cannot be asked to follow with our own eyes. And indeed, the poet's language still contradicts it, speaking of the appearance of the rose, its colour and breadth, the faces of angels and the countenances of the blest. But such language continues to appear for somewhat the same reason Dante invokes to explain why the Scriptures assign a human-like body to God[47]: it is a language of accommodation, permitting the reader

[42] XXVI, 79   [43] XXX, 58   [44] XXX, 78
[45] XXX, 88–89   [46] XXX, 91–92   [47] Cf. IV, 40 ff.

to grasp at least the nature, at least the direction, of the experience which—as experience—lies outside his reach. Recognizing that the poem must either become silent at this point or else adopt the language of common reality, Dante makes the only choice possible to him. But we *know* that the faces and the petals of the rose which we imagine under sensuous form are not there at all in such form. They are in the pilgrim's mind. They are akin perhaps to what Kant calls *intellectual* or *original* perceptions, unmediated by time or space. The strongest proof that this is what Dante intends lies less in his repeated protests that he cannot tell what he saw than in the sudden, astonishing re-emergence of simple recognizability in the appearances of the blest. Heretofore all had been dazzling sparks of light. But St Bernard, appearing in Beatrice's place at the pilgrim's side as the rose comes to view, is *an elder clad like the folk in glory. His eyes and cheeks were overpoured with benign gladness, in kindly gesture as befits a tender father.*[48] And from here on each member of the host is recognized at a glance.

It follows that God, too, if seen at all, must be seen by direct intellectual perception, without sensuous intermediation. And what else can be meant by such language as: *my sight, becoming purged, now more and more was entering through the ray of the deep light which in itself is true*[49]? What else (when the pilgrim fixes his eyes on the supreme light) can be meant by: *Thenceforward was my vision mightier than our discourse, which faileth at such sight, and faileth memory at so great outrage*[50]? God is witnessed as light, yes—but light shorn of every physical attribute, light as an intellectual percept, and thus in a way quite unavailable to mortal minds. And yet—the poem can do what no reasoning could do. It has crammed and crowded the reader's mind with images of light, dazzled him out of sensuous response; so that what remains is the idea of light without specific form, and he can by the analogy of this experience move towards some fleeting

[48] XXXI, 59–63   [49] XXXIII, 52–54   [50] XXXIII, 55–57

sense of what it might be to be suffused with truth, yet not to see, feel, taste, touch or smell.

We come at this point in the narrative of the *Comedy* to the second of the two great images which divide the *Paradiso's* theme between them, and which begin and end the canticle. In it the poet records the final and culminating vision of pure light and of the totality and unity of being. Bound in the *volume* of that light are the contents of universal creation: the *scattered leaves of all the universe, substance and accidents and their relations as though together fused*, the *universal form of this complex*. What are we to understand by this miraculous summary? The light, we know, is God; and God, according to Dante's theology, is an unmoved mover, receiving nothing whatsoever from without. But Dante's image does not contradict this. God is an eternal *mirror* of his own radiance reflected back from every member of the creation. He is the *point whereto all times are present*.[51] Since his being is outside the dimension of time, there is no before or after in him, therefore his creative act and the response of his creatures throughout all time are, in his eternal dimension, simultaneous. Since his being is not in space, there is no *place* in him, and he is in no place; therefore all created things are, in his spaceless dimension, real yet without concrete form, and coexistent. He is *Alpha and Omega, the beginning and the ending*, both as men conceive these—in a series—and as he himself does, with no lapse whatever between. As light he sends forth the creative ray that sets up the temporal-spatial universe and illumines it. As light he mirrors eternally the totality of the result.

The stress in the whole final canto falls clearly on the mystery of the many in the one, as in the earlier parts of the canticle it fell on the issuing of the one into multiplicity. In the flame of the final vision the pilgrim sees gathered the scattered leaves of all the universe, the total record of all that tends towards being and all that achieves it, fused into a flawless, simple whole. In the flame the

[51] XVII, 17–18

universe is resumed without seam or break, freed of its delusive extensions in time and space; the strewn puzzle is assembled, the harmony of all its fragments established. If the flame is God in his totality and simplicity, the *gathered leaves* are the presence in him of that Idea which he expatiates in the creation. The pilgrim, gazing at the one in the other, stands in the presence of that towards which the whole cure of his eyes has been directed: that *good of the intellect* which those in Hell have lost, the primal Truth from which all men's splinter truths derive and by which in turn they must be measured. He comes to this vision of wholeness, as the story has told us, after the bitterest experience of wrong seeing, loss of way, miraculous aid, and a journey that regenerates the mind's eyes. A glimpse is all he gets—or needs. The vision breaks. He is returned to the world as a homing pilgrim in whom *desire and will* are now *rolled* by divine love *even as a wheel that moveth equally*.

Thus the pilgrim becomes again the poet; the poet who was the pilgrim is ready to write down the story and the sense of his journey; and the wheel-shaped *Comedy* of Dante Alighieri begins again.

SUGGESTED READINGS

The following brief bibliography has been compiled for the reader who may wish to pursue the study of Dante further, and in other directions. Foreign-language works are listed exclusively in English translations wherever possible, except in the case of Dante's writings and French and Italian lyric poetry.

I. WORKS BY DANTE

La Divina Commedia: the best standard Italian edition is that of the Società Dantesca Italiana, with copious notes and commentary by Scartazzini and Vandelli. This is revised and reissued at frequent intervals by Hoepli at Milan.

Le Opere: testo critico della Società Dantesca Italiana, Florence, 1921.

Le Rime (ed. Gianfranco Contini). Turin, 1946.

Complete works in English translation, with the original printed on facing pages, except in the case of the Latin works: in five volumes, Temple Classics edition. London and New York.

II. CRITICISM AND AIDS TO CRITICISM

Auerbach, Erich: *Dante, Poet of the Secular World*, transl. by R. Manheim. University of Chicago Press, 1961.

—— "Figura" in *Scenes from the Drama of European Literature*, transl. by R. Manheim. Meridian Books, New York, 1959.

—— *Mimesis*, transl. by W. Trask. Princeton University Press, 1953.

Bodkin, Maude: *Archetypal Patterns in Poetry*. Vintage Books, New York, 1958.

Coomaraswamy, Ananda K.: "Figures of Speech or Figures of Thought?" in volume of the same title. Luzac & Co., Ltd., London, 1946.

Croce, Benedetto: *The Poetry of Dante*, transl. by D. Ainslee. Henry Holt, New York, 1922.

De Sanctis, Francesco: *Esposizione Critica della Divina Commedia*. Naples, 1921.

Di Pino, Guido: *La Figurazione della Luce nella Divina Commedia*. Florence, 1952.

Dunbar, H. Flanders: *Symbolism in Medieval Thought*. Yale University Press, 1929.

Eliot, T. S.: "Dante" in *Selected Essays*. Harcourt, Brace, New York, 1932.

Fergusson, Francis: *Dante's Drama of the Mind*. Princeton University Press, 1953.

Fletcher, Jefferson B.: *Symbolism of the Divine Comedy*. Columbia University Press, 1921.

Gardner, Edmund: *Dante's Ten Heavens*. Constable & Co., Ltd., London, 1900.

—— *Dante and the Mystics*. Dutton, New York, 1913.

Malagoli, Luigi: *Linguaggio e poesia nella Divina Commedia*. Genoa, 1949.

Maritain, Jacques: "Dante's Innocence and Luck" in *Kenyon Review*. Gambier, Ohio, Spring, 1952.

Moore, Edward: *Studies in Dante* (in four series). Clarendon Press, Oxford, 1896–1917.

Santayana, George: *Three Philosophical Poets*. Harvard University Press, 1910.

Singleton, Charles: *An Essay on the Vita Nuova*. Harvard University Press, 1949.

—— *Commedia: Elements of Structure*. Harvard University Press, 1954.

—— *Journey to Beatrice*. Harvard University Press, 1958.

Stambler, Bernard: *Dante's Other World*. New York University Press, 1957.

Toynbee, Paget: *Dante Studies and Researches*. Milford, Oxford, 1921.

Wicksteed, Philip: *Dante and Aquinas*. Dutton, New York, 1913.

—— *From Vita Nuova to Paradiso*. Longmans & Co., Ltd., London, 1922.

III. HISTORY, BIOGRAPHY, MEDIEVAL CULTURE

Asin, Miguel: *Islam and the Divine Comedy*, transl. by H. Sunderland. John Murray, London, 1926.

Barbi, Michele: *Life of Dante*, transl. by P. Ruggiers, University of California Press, 1954.

Compagni, Dino: *The Chronicle*, transl. by E. C. M. Benecke and A. C. F. Howell. Dutton, New York, n.d.

Curtius, Ernst: *European Literature and the Latin Middle Ages*, transl. by W. Trask. Pantheon Books, New York, 1953.

de Rougemont, Denis: *Love in the Western World*, transl. by M. Belgion. Pantheon Books, New York, 1956.

Gilson, Etienne: *The Spirit of Medieval Philosophy*, transl. by A. H. C. Downes. Charles Scribner's Sons, New York, 1936.

—— *The Philosophy of St. Thomas Aquinas*, transl. by E. Bullough. Herder, St. Louis, 1937.

Graf, Arturo: *Miti, Leggende e Superstizioni del Medio Evo*. Turin, 1892.

Hirn, Yrjo: *The Sacred Shrine*. Macmillan & Co., Ltd., London, 1912.

Lewis, C. S.: *The Allegory of Love*. Galaxy Books, New York, 1958.

Mâle, Emile: *Religious Art in France, XIII Century*, transl. by D. Nussey. Dutton, New York, 1913.

Maury, Alfred: *Croyances et Légendes du Moyen Age*. Paris, 1896.

Patch, Howard R.: *The Other World*, according to de-

scriptions in medieval literature. Harvard University
Press, 1950.

Renucci, Paul: *L'aventure de l'humanisme européen au
moyen âge*. Paris, 1953.

Schevill, Ferdinand: *History of Florence*. Harcourt, Brace,
New York, 1936.

Taylor, Henry Osborn: *The Mediaeval Mind*. Macmillan,
New York, 1925.

Von Simson, Otto: *The Gothic Cathedral*. Pantheon
Books, New York, 1956.

Vossler, Karl: *Medieval Culture: An Introduction to
Dante and his Times*, transl. by W. C. Lawton. Harcourt, Brace, New York, 1929.

Wicksteed, Philip: *The Early Lives of Dante*. King's Classics, De La More Press, London, 1904.

IV. A FEW OF DANTE'S SOURCES

Aquinas, Thomas: *Basic Writings*, ed. by A. Pegis. Random House, New York, 1945.

Aristotle: *Basic Works*, ed. by R. McKeon. Random
House, New York, 1941.

Augustine, St: *The City of God*, transl. by John Healy.
Dutton, New York, 1931.

—— *The Confessions*, transl. by E. B. Pusey. Dutton,
New York, 1910.

Bernard, St: *On the Love of God*, in Vol. XIII, Library
of Christian Classics (ed. by Ray C. Petry). Westminster Press, Philadelphia, 1957.

Boethius: *In Consolation of Philosophy*, transl. by W. V.
Cooper. Random House, New York, 1943.

Bonaventura, St: *The Journey of the Mind to God*, in Vol.
XIII, Library of Christian Classics (ed. by Ray C.
Petry). Westminster Press, Philadelphia, 1957.

Ovid: *The Metamorphoses*, transl. by Rolfe Humphries,
Indiana University Press, Bloomington, 1955.

Plato: *The Timaeus*, transl. with commentary by F. M.
Cornford in *Plato's Cosmology*. Liberal Arts Press,
New York, 1957.

Virgil: *The Aeneid*, transl. by Rolfe Humphries. Charles
Scribner's Sons, New York, 1958.

French and Italian lyric poetry in anthologies:

Anglade, Joseph: *Anthologie des Troubadours*. Paris,
1927.

Guerrieri Crocetti, C.: *La Lirica Predantesca*. Florence, 1925.

Rossetti, D. G.: *The Early Italian Poets*. London and
New York, n.d. (The Muses' Library).

Waddell, Helen: *Mediaeval Latin Lyrics*. Constable
& Co., Ltd., London, 1929.

ANCHOR BOOKS

DOLPHIN BOOKS AND DOLPHIN MASTERS

The bold face M indicates a Dolphin Master. Dolphin Masters are Dolphin Books in the editions of greatest importance to the teacher and student. In selecting the Dolphin Masters, the editors have taken particular pains to choose copies of the most significant edition (usually the first) by obtaining original books or their facsimiles or by having reproductions made of library copies of particularly rare editions. Facsimiles of original title pages and other appropriate material from the first edition are included in many Masters.

FICTION

A-240872-pa 23
(2 bks)